Measure of People and Space Interactions in the Built Environment

Towards Responsive Development

Edited by

Abubakar Danladi Isah

Federal University of Technology Minna, Nigeria

Isa Bala Muhammad

Federal University of Technology Minna, Nigeria

Series in Built Environment

VERNON PRESS

www.vernonpress.com

In the Americas:
Vernon Press
1000 N West Street,
Suite 1200, Wilmington,
Delaware 19801
United States

In the rest of the world:
Vernon Press
C/Sancti Espiritu 17,
Malaga, 29006
Spain

Series in Built Environment

Library of Congress Control Number: 2018951007

ISBN: 978-1-62273-710-9

Also available:

Hardback: 978-1-62273-442-9

E-book: 978-1-62273-555-6

Cover design by Vernon Press, using elements selected by freepik.

Table of contents

Foreword

This is a book that took me completely by surprise for two main reasons; first it concerns a subject matter that is not for the casual reader because it is complex and intangible, and secondly and more importantly it is by a group of Nigerian doctorate holders who graduated less than 5 years ago. In the Nigerian context this is extremely unusual and unprecedented. Every year I suspect hundreds if not thousands of Nigerians are awarded doctorate degrees from home and abroad which end up in library shelves and whatever knowledge these contain are lost to Nigeria and Nigerians. While some of these works never get disseminated because the researchers may not consider them much to write home about, others never get to see the light of day because the researchers simply never inculcated the academic spirit. Yet many of these works are extremely good and contain insights that could lead to breakthroughs in many fields. In addition, they could serve as inspiration for many researchers old and new. It is in this light that this book deserves praise and admiration. Here is a group that is thinking out of the box, that have started publishing their research works even before the ink on their doctorates is dry.

The focus of the book is, 'people and space interactions in different settings'. Each of the seven chapters of the book touches on one aspect or the other of this vast field. The book deals with cultural landscapes, sustainable housing settings, the environment and human response, spatial epidemiology, neighbourhood and health, and the subjectivity-objectivity continuum in man-environment research. From the foregoing, it is obvious that various disciplines are touched and those to benefit from the work include, but not restricted to scholars of geography, anthropology, sociology, urban planning, architecture, and above all environment-behaviour studies.

What is unique about the work is not the number of disciplines touched upon nor the numerous subject matters but what unites these diverse issues besides the focus on human relationship and response to the environment, and that is most of the authors are architects. The reason is simple; architects at least in Nigeria if not in Africa tend to downplay the academic aspects of architecture and over-emphasise the practical aspect of design. The end result is that architecture in Nigeria lacks theoretical depth and consequently, it tends towards an architecture without élan vital or panache. Thus, the book should be a demonstration of the possibility of uniting theory and practice in the profession of architecture. Furthermore, it is a first step toward focusing on an architecture for the people at least, if not by them or of them; how it is read, how it is interpreted and how meaning can be made out of a subject matter that can be complex and even complicated.

In conclusion, one would like to state that the form and hence the orientation of the people and space interactions may differ but the underlying structure and hence the function remain valid for all the cases here. All one needs is the ability to see beyond the form and the orientation of the different approaches to the importance of the structure and the universals which could lead to the basis for drawing meanings in comparisons.

A. A. Muhammad-Oumar
Bayero University, Kano
KANO   October 2017

Preface

Research contributions relating various aspects of research methodology abound in several disciplines. However, research methodologies related to specific phenomenon in several disciplines are rare. The essence of this book is to identify and fill such gap by relating appropriate scientific structure of inquiry with respect to certain phenomena in the built environment.

Significantly, the methodological framework presented in the various chapters of this book relates to the Sustainable Development Goals advocated by the United Nations. It also aligns with the United Nations' concept of sustainable development of physical landscape and living spaces as inhabitants interrelate with their settlements.

The book concentrates on the "Measurement" approach- which involves identification of variables relating people and space, as well as applying principally suitable data sources and analyses methods in order to develop an "Assessment" tool- for performance evaluation based on existing criterion or established criteria.

Thus, this book contributes towards an appropriate approach in measuring people and space interactions in different settings that include tourist wellbeing in a typical hilly landscape, disease management patterns with spatial structure in urban neighbourhoods. Others are healthcare facilities, housing studies and cultural landscape of typical ethnic settlement. All these aforementioned examples of people-space interactions are subsumed into a collection- towards projecting appropriate path for researchers interested in mainstream values of people and their environment. Most importantly is that each chapter made up of different studies which related people and space transactions in resolving global challenges of sustainable and responsive habitations in both urban and rural environments. Apart from targeting researchers and professionals in the built environment, this book may appeal to sociologist and anthropologists.

Abubakar Danladi Isah PhD   Minna, Nigeria 2017

Chapter contributions

Chapter One

This book is an attempt to introduce various research methods and strategies that can be used in social research, taking human interaction with its environment as its main focus. The inclination of research towards various levels of objectivity or subjectivity opens up room for discussion on how social research that involves human as subjects can belong to almost any level in the continuum. That is quite a significant contribution in a way that social researchers continue to get support and feel confident to break free from obliging strictly to total objectivity or subjectivity.

Tareef Hayat Khan PhD

Universiti Tecknologi Malaysia

Chapter Two

So far, no previous study has investigated the restorative benefits of contact with mountain landscape environment. Therefore, extensive research remains to be carried out in the investigation of the mechanism and intricacies of the link between restorative environments, human response and wellbeing. Hence, a synergetic approach in the measurement of the psycho-physiological responses of individuals within a real-life multi-stimulus mountain landscape environment is required. This is in order to further extend research in the environment and human well-being domain.

Henry Ojobo PhD

Kaduna State University, Kaduna, Nigeria

Chapter Three

The neighbourhoods with negative parameter estimates of diseases are in the areas with significant t-values which indicate the influence of urbanization. This is because the influence of urbanization on Meningococcal meningitis, for instance, is on the inverse, implying that the less the urbanization, then the more the influence of the disease in those neighbourhoods. Thus, having an understanding of the spatial and temporal changes of diseases and categorizing the spatial structure was the central point of this chapter more so the importance of spatial structures of diseases for health planners as the population interact with their environment.

Emmanuel Umaru Tanko PhD

Federal University of Technology Minna, Nigeria

Chapter Four

The combination of several strategies in investigating patient and family relationship demonstrates that various methods are used in different fields of study and can fuse together towards building a framework for another scientific inquiry. The sequential and parallel order by which such investigation is scheduled shows some rigour in the approach used for data elicitation. Most importantly, findings evolving from such process are valid and reliable due to its multi-dimensional trail.

Ibrahim Abubakar Alkali PhD

Bayero University Kano, Nigeria

Chapter Five

Systematically, sustainable housing research better combines various settings as a result of diverse human and ethnic commonalities while seeking the understanding of physical setting and inhabitants' behaviour. The operational methodology appropriate is a qualitative research that adopts a multi-case studies strategy, with multi-phase sampling technique using a mixed-method approach in data eliciting and processing as well as in the interpretation.

Abubakar Danladi Isah PhD

Federal University of Technology Minna, Nigeria

Chapter Six

Cultural landscape study showcases the extensive step by step process involved in the elicitation of cultural landscape values of communities. These, amongst others, include the formation of rapport with the study community, the use of multi-method approach in the elicitation of data about the indigenous people upon which the bedrock of the information was ethnographic. The ethnographic process allowed for data to be gathered and understood through the perspective of the indigenous people.

Isa Bala Muhammad PhD

Federal University of Technology Minna, Nigeria

Chapter Seven

The scientific procedure for conducting research in people and space transactions is characterised with a plethora of approaches which most of the time could be confusing especially to a beginner researcher. This book significantly provided measures of people and space interactions in the built environment towards responsive development. It covers the consideration of different settings of the built environment that include mountainous landscape, urban neighbourhood, hospital built environment, public housing setting and cultural landscape of a typical rural ethnic community. These settings are influenced by culture and technology in space optimisation, linking urban dynamics with mainstream indigenous cultural values in both tangible and intangible expressions. In this regard, researchers move towards thinking out of the box and identifying appropriate methodology, which means they encounter new innovative and creative methodologies that better fit the phenomenon under investigation.

Isa Bala Muhammad PhD

Abubakar Danladi Isah PhD

Federal University of Technology Minna, Nigeria

About the book editors

Abubakar Danladi Isah PhD

Abubakar Danladi Isah was awarded a PhD in Architecture by the Universiti Teknologi Malaysia. He also holds a bachelor's honour degree in Architecture and a master's degree in the same discipline from the Federal University of Technology Minna, Nigeria. He is a registered architect and has practiced for several years engaging in housing and institutional buildings' design and construction. With several years of teaching experience, he has worked as a visiting lecturer and facilitated research inputs in many universities. He has written several journal articles, a book chapter and has authored the book, 'Urban Public Housing in Northern Nigeria: The Search for Indigeneity and Cultural Practices in Design'. His research interests include space use and human behaviour, building and culture, sustainable housing, research methods, and ethics and moral reformation.

Abubakar Danladi Isah is also a reviewer for several local and international journals, conferences and an Editorial member of the Archi-Culture Journal at the University of Jos, Nigeria. He has attended training courses in human ethics and peaceful co-existence which qualify him as a human moral reform consultant. Thus, his academic and practical experience in leadership and participation in public presentations has allowed him to fully understand how people interact with and understand their environment.

Isa Bala Muhammad PhD

Isa Bala Muhammad obtained his PhD in Architecture from the Universiti Teknologi Malaysia and was the recipient of the best graduating PhD student Award in the Department of Architecture in 2015. He received his Master's Degree as well as Bachelor's degree in architecture in 2000 and 2002 respectively from the Federal University of Technology Minna, Nigeria. He joined the services of the Niger State government as an architect in 2003 where he designed and supervised several projects and later rose to the position of senior architect. He later joined the Federal University of Technology Minna as a lecturer in 2007 and has lectured and supervised both undergraduate and post-graduate students. He has written several research articles and a book, on cultural landscape. His research interests are Ethnography, Cultural landscapes, Ecosystem Services & Human Behaviour, and Environment.

Isa Bala Muhammad is a reviewer of University-based journals including the Pertanika Journal of Science and Technology, Universiti of Putra Malaysia; the Archi-Culture Journal, University of Jos Nigeria and the Nigerian Journal of Technological Research, Federal University of Technology Minna. He is also an Editorial member of the Environmental Technology and Science Journal at the Federal University of Technology Minna. Additionally, he is a registered member of Teachers Registration Council of Nigeria and Architect's Registration Council of Nigeria.

Chapter 1

Introduction

Tareef Hayat Khan

Department of Architecture, Faculty of Built Environment,

Universiti Tecknologi Malaysia

tareef@utm.edu.my, roopak23@gmail.com

Adoption of a suitable scale of measurement in the evaluation of a research phenomenon is significant in determining the validity and reliability of the process as well as its outcome. Systematically this book focuses on the scientific procedure of some selected phenomena in people and space transactions in the built environment. Remarkably, the development of the chapters is guided by the focus on sustainability and responsiveness of research process and outcomes in order to enhance global and contextual goals of UN sustainable development goals (SDGs). Therefore, the book presents methods and research focused on appropriate measures geared towards sustainability in the benefits of human interactions with both their indoor and outdoor (space and landscape) environments with regards to the consideration of mainstream values in ensuring liveability and sustainability in an urban environment. Consequently, a multi-dimensional strategy seems to be appropriate in measuring the relationship and interaction between inhabitants and their (urban) environment.

Research is about a systematic approach to solve problems. Research outcomes are aimed at contributing to human wellbeing. When the methods of achieving research outcomes are documented comprehensively it not only provides help to other researchers to replicate it in order to gain same or similar outcome, perhaps in a broader scale, but it also provides a basic platform for further research into that particular or similar issues. Proper documentation of research methods and its inherent strategies also provide new researchers to challenge an outcome in one way, or to reinforce the method in another way. It is all about transparency so that researchers around the world can take help from fellow other researchers as much as possible and can act as a single community aiming for that same goal – contribute to human wellbeing.

However, methods vary from research to research depending on the onto-logical differences. The research topic can provide the researcher with the first question: Which paradigm do I belong to for this research? This is be-cause the research methodology and the subsequent developed strategies are easier to be determined when a paradigm is chosen for research. While there are positivist and interpretivist paradigms on the two extremes that are tradi-tionally supported by quantitative and qualitative methods respectively, modern researchers argue that in any paradigm, methods can be mixed, which infers that different objectives in the research might adopt different quantitative and qualitative methods and strategies in order to achieve the aim of the research. In a way, it liberates the researcher not to be forced into quantitative or qualitative methods strictly along the whole journey of the research. In another way, it also acknowledges the limitations of both meth-ods in order to address the reality. The reality itself can, therefore, be recog-nized as neither total objectivity nor total subjectivity, but somewhere in be-tween. It may not be comfortable for all researchers, but for social research-ers, where humans are the subject matter, most probably that kind of reality is acceptable. It is not only because every human subject is different, and there-fore, a total objective reality is absolutely unattainable, but also because the researcher is also a human being, and probably susceptible in interpreting outcomes in a way that can be acceptable to every reader. Therefore, 'proba-bility' plays a very important role in social research. Depending on the re-search topic, the probability of the acceptance of research outcomes may be higher or lower. That is why the research methodology becomes more im-portant for social research as more transparency can lead to more acceptabil-ity, or at least can lead to fair criticism.

Focusing on the research topic of this book in which human interaction with its environment is the ontological domain, there could be different re-search areas that are inclined to different levels of Objectivity and Subjectivity. Relating quantitative methods with objectivity and qualitative methods with subjectivity, Morgan and Smircich (1980) tried to show how research ap-proaches can belong to a range in a continuum, rather than simple discretely identifiable levels. Joroff and Morse (1984) even showed which types of re-search could lie on which particular range in a subjective-objective continu-um. That opened up the debate even more nicely for social research, and allowed social researchers to try different methods to different extents, and let the skill and stance of the researcher to convince the reader about the out-come of the research to be acceptable in the bigger knowledge base.

While arguably more scientific, and hence, more quantitative methods such as laboratory experiments could be used to study human interaction with environmental factors (example: as daylight, heat, etc.), pure qualitative methods such as ethnography are preferred to study cultural factors (example: human behaviour, cultural traits, etc.). Considering these at almost two extreme ends for research topics related to human interaction with its environment, in between may lie many research areas which might demand a varied level of objectivity and subjectivity. It is important for the researcher to understand which research area should belong to which level in the continuum. Therefore, the idea of putting together five different research topics in this book where these five lie on different levels in that continuum was definitely interesting.

The methods used to measure the human wellbeing in Mountain landscape environment clearly adopted the quantitative methods as stated in the research methodology. However, all the parameters were not purely quantifiable. For example, even though mountain environment (that include river, forest, waterfall, etc.) could be clearly defined, the ambient environment conditions that include temperature, humidity, etc.) could be quantifiable, and even human physiological responses (that include blood pressure, pulse rate, respiratory rate, etc.) could be quantifiable, human psychological perception (that include stress, excitement, calmness) were not. That created room for subjectivity in this research, especially while establishing relationships between the variables. Therefore, one can assume that this research belongs to somewhere in the middle of the continuum, and though not at the objective end, it may be more inclined towards that direction.

The study of control and management of epidemics through spatial statistical analysis is another good example to investigate a subjective research area with a more objective research tool. The parameters were quite measurable, for example, the location of the hospital, location of the refuse dump, the house conditions, population's density, ownership pattern, etc. However, the tools used such as Getis and Ords hot spatial analysis, Geographically Weighted Regression, and Spatial Pattern Analysis are based on statistical probability. Moreover, the sample collection method might also have had significant level of subjectivity, and therefore, this research could well belong close to the middle of the continuum, even though there are efforts to incline it towards objectivity.

The research on designing strategy for inpatient wards by examining hospital spaces and family care action has adopted self-proclaimed qualitative methods, where the researcher depended on interactive interviews and observation for data collection. Behaviour mapping technics were qualitative methods of analysis, and intense logical argumentation was necessary to justify the outcomes. The outcomes, in this case, were design strategies, which were also qualitative in nature. Moreover, the researcher's background might also have significantly affected the argumentation. However, the research topic gave room to generalize the findings, as health care strategies have been standardized to a certain extent throughout the world. Therefore, even though qualitative methods were adopted, the research does not necessarily belong to the extreme end of subjectivity in the continuum, though more inclined towards that direction, and most probably in a balanced situation near the middle.

The final two topics by their titles indicate to belong in the subjective half in the continuum. In Chapter 5, determining cultural attributes of a particular community was the foremost task of the researcher which is hard to be based on any quantitative methods. The methods included participant observation, Gamma diagram, Qualitative Factor Analysis at different stages of data collection and analysis. These are all qualitative in nature. Thereafter, using the cultural attributes in order to determine the culture responsive design needed strong context specific background of the researcher, as well as a long-term involvement with the community. The findings, therefore, tend strongly towards the subjective end in the continuum.

In Chapter 6, the significant parameters that were measured were cultural values and community values. There are purely qualitative in nature, and very difficult to generalize. The method was ethnography, where the researcher needed to stay with the community for a considerable time period in order to convince the reader that all the parameters of the research had been comprehended at a significant level. Therefore, validation of the research becomes less important, and trustworthiness becomes more significant. That is why the research became inclined to the subjective end very distinctively.

Therefore, this book is an attempt to introduce various research methods and strategies that can be used in social research, taking human interaction with its environment as its main focus. Their inclination towards various levels of objectivity or subjectivity opens up room for discussion on how social research that involves human as subjects can belong to almost any level in the continuum. That is a quite significant contribution in a way that social researchers continue to get support and feel confident to break free from obliging strictly to total objectivity or subjectivity.

References

Morgan, G. & Smircich, L. (1980) The Case for Qualitative research. *The Academy of Management Review* (pre-1986). Briarcliff Manor, 5, 491-500.

Joroff, M. & Morse, S. (1984) A Proposed Framework for the Emerging Field of Architectural Research. *Architectural Research*, 15-24.

Chapter 2

Multidimensional assessment strategy of human wellbeing in mountain landscape environment Obudu, Nigeria

Henry Ojobo

Department of Architecture, Kaduna State University, Kaduna, Nigeria

ojheny@gmail.com

Abstract: With regards to the link between nature experience and wellbeing, the bene-fits of contact with a mountain landscape environment on psycho-physiological states are explored. A basic assumption guiding research in this area relates to how cumula-tive effects of contact with environments having restorative qualities can enhance human wellbeing more than those without restorative qualities. Therefore, aspects of this assumption in relation to mountain landscape environments involve visual and physical interaction, psycho-physiological response and the span of time required for cumulative effects of restorative experience to manifest. This chapter describes the multiple inter-related research design employed in order to elicit data on the benefits of human contact with the mountain landscape environment with regards to the en-hancement of human wellbeing. A quantitative methodological approach was em-ployed to explore the full range of psychological and physiological aspects of human wellbeing. It involved cross-sectional and interrupted time-series between group exper-imental surveys. This was based on a cause and effect phenomenon comparing contact with the urban and mountain landscape environment. Respondents from the urban population co-opted through random convenience sampling method were engaged in both the cross-sectional and interrupted time-series within group experimental survey. The study utilized psychometric questionnaires, physical measures of physiological indices and instrumented measures of ambient environment conditions to elicit data.

Keywords: Wellbeing; Mountain Landscape; Nature; Restoration; Obudu

Introduction

The quest for attainment of physical and mental wellbeing through alterna-tive medicine is a universal human goal. Quite a number of studies have been carried out on the effects of nature experience on mental wellbeing (Bratman *et al.*, 2012; Kaplan, 1992; Russell *et al.*, 2013; Ulrich, 1979). A key element of the health benefits of nature may be its stress reducing effect. However, stress can be assessed from an inexhaustible perspective. In healthcare manage-ment, stress is vital in considering the etiology of diverse common health challenges which include cardiovascular diseases, anxiety disorders, obesity and depression (Lee and Oh, 2010; Probst, 2013). In landscape studies, stress is viewed in terms of the contribution of urbanization, lifestyle changes and the ameliorating potentials of nature related environments (Hartig *et al.*, 2014). Generally, various researchers have tried to conceptualize the negative attributes of stress (e.g. forgetfulness, distractions, mistakes and illness) and also critically assess the positive aspects of restoration linked to nature (e.g. feeling relaxed, effectiveness, productivity and wellbeing) (Bergdahl and Bergdahl, 2002; Kaplan, 2001a; Kaplan and Kaplan, 2011; Tsunetsugu *et al.*, 2013). Meanwhile, the apparent detachment of most individuals from nature has contributed to their stress and disease state. Hence, the proponents of nature oriented psychotherapy have advanced explanations concerning health effects of natural environments with the intent of linking the man-nature versus wellbeing paradigm.

On the whole, the body of knowledge has expanded with researchers explor-ing more on the psycho-physiological benefits of interacting with varying real forest environments using multiple measures (Horiuchi *et al.*, 2014; Ochiai *et al.*, 2015; Tsunetsugu *et al.*, 2013). Agreeably, whilst quite a number of studies have been carried out on the restorative benefits of forests and wilderness environments, mountain landscape environments have received little atten-tion. Researchers situating mountain landscape environments as study con-text have focused more on estimating visual properties and aesthetic values with regards to preference and perception (Beza, 2010; Lindemann-Matthies *et al.*, 2010; Schirpke *et al.*, 2013a; Schirpke *et al.*, 2013b; Tveit, 2009).

So far, no previous study has investigated the restorative benefits of contact with mountain landscape environment. Therefore, extensive research re-mains to be carried out in the investigation of the mechanism and intricacies of the link between restorative environments, human response and wellbeing. Hence, a synergetic approach in the measurement of the psycho-physiological responses of individuals within a real-life multi-stimulus moun-tain landscape environment is required. This is in order to further extend research in the environment and human well-being domain. The Obudu mountain landscape environment in Nigeria, endowed with rich, multi-stimulus landscape features offered a veritable platform for this study.

The methodology engaged in this study focused on measuring the benefits of human contact with the mountain landscape environment with regards to restoration of directed attention and stress mitigation. Thus, a multi-dimensional cause and effect strategy comparing contact with the urban environment and mountain landscape environment was elucidated. This chapter, therefore, describes the research design and the methods applied to elicit the data to achieve the foregoing.

Research Approach and Paradigm

Research paradigm involves the philosophical dimensions comprising the basic beliefs and assumptions about the world and technical dimensions comprising the methods and technique adopted when conducting research (McGregor and Murnane, 2010). Paramount to this study was the examination of the link between restorative environments, human response and wellbeing in a mountain landscape environment. Thus, the school of thought reflecting the process of scenic-quality assessment and the determination of the causes that influence effects or outcome was considered most appropriate.

To adequately achieve the goal of the study, a multiple paradigm approach was utilized (Hall, 2012). Therefore, three compatible paradigms as shown in Figure 2.1 namely, psychophysical, experiential and post-positivistic para-digm formed a tripartite support with which the study was situated.

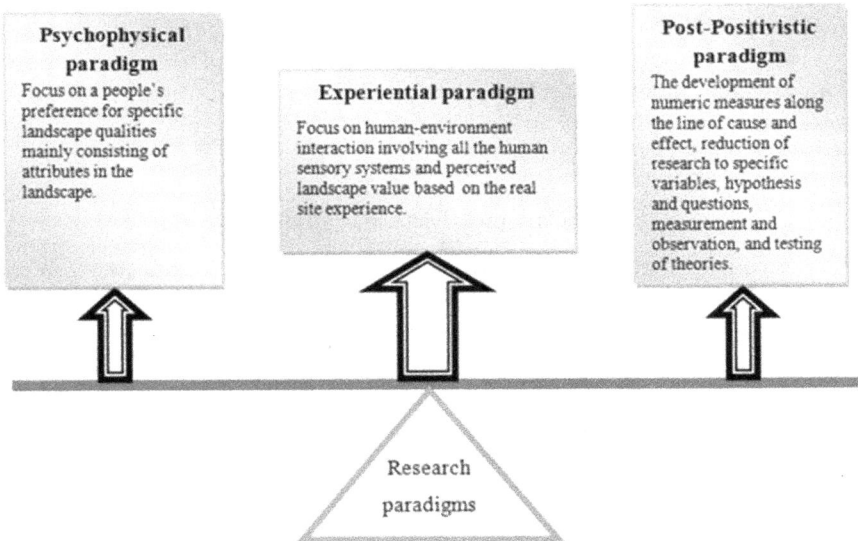

Psychophysical paradigm
Focus on a people's preference for specific landscape qualities mainly consisting of attributes in the landscape.

Experiential paradigm
Focus on human-environment interaction involving all the human sensory systems and perceived landscape value based on the real site experience.

Post-Positivistic paradigm
The development of numeric measures along the line of cause and effect, reduction of research to specific variables, hypothesis and questions, measurement and observation, and testing of theories.

Research paradigms

Figure 2.1 Philosophical dimensions of human-environment interaction

Psychophysical and Experiential Paradigms

In evaluating scenic or visual landscape quality in a real environment, the psychophysical and experiential paradigm is considered. While the psychophysical paradigm focuses on a population's preference for specific landscape qualities mainly consisting physical attributes in the landscape, the experiential paradigm is hinged on landscape values based on the people's interaction with the landscape (Deming and Swaffield, 2011). The psychophysical paradigm entails only the visual aspects of preference (Kroh and Gimblett, 1992) while the experiential involves the use of all the human sensory systems. In other words, the psychophysical paradigm assumes that landscapes have stimulating attributes which are external to the individual. On the other hand, the experiential paradigm is hinged on the human-environment interaction and perceived landscape value based on the experience (Kaymaz, 2012b).

However, it is important to state that the traditional view of experiential paradigm only takes into consideration the psychological aspects of human-environment interaction relative to landscape perception. The method for this study modifies that view by adding the physiological aspects of human-environment interaction relative to physiological responses of individuals. Therefore, in investigating the benefits and extent of the mountain landscape environment on individual perception, psychological and physiological responses, it was necessary to adopt the psychophysical and experiential paradigms. In this study, psychological assessment of individuals provided the knowledge of an individual's perceptual pattern and behaviour towards the mountain landscape environment. And, the physiological assessment provided the information on individual responses based on human anatomical indices of stress.

Post-positivistic Paradigm

Post-positivistic paradigm is primarily based on the world view which amends the inadequacy of positivism, a paradigm simply based on facts identification combined with measurable entities (Lather, 1992). Post-positivism involves the development of numeric measures along the line of cause and effect, reduction of research to specific variables, hypothesis and questions, measurement and observation, and testing of theories (Creswell, 2013). The idea is often associated with quantitative or empirical research methods and entails the investigation of a phenomenon from theory to hypotheses or questions down to data modifying or contradicting the theory (Creswell and Clark, 2007). In empirical research, observations and behaviour are ascertained through measurements and experimentation (Krauss, 2005). Thus, the approach of this study emphasizes the post-positivistic point of view in terms of methods of enquiry and measurements. Through the direct measurements of the psychological and physiological phenomenon of human-environment interaction in a mountain landscape environment it applied the cause and effect strategy.

The Study Perspectives and Derivation of Research Queries

The study was accessed from three perspectives dealing with the potentials of a restorative environment relative to human response and wellbeing in a mountain landscape environment. The first perspective pertains to environmental preference and perception based on subjective psychological responses. Environmental preference is closely related to restoration and is accessed by the presence of attributes within the environment that is perceived by the individual as having a potential functional significance (Van den Berg *et al.*, 2003). In other words, the perception of individuals concerning features present in an environment is linked to restoration and wellbeing. Based on this notion, the first research question RQ1 was formulated. RQ1 sought to identify the features (e.g. fountains, water bodies, greenery and plant material) of the mountain environment that provides restorative benefits in terms of preference and perception.

The second perspective involved both psychological and physiological aspects of experiential contact with the mountain landscape environment. The assumption guiding research in this area involves the comparison of the effects of contact with environments possessing restorative qualities than those without it (Hartig, *et al.*, 2011). Determining the difference in experience, therefore, entails the comparison between the stimulating effects of urban and mountain landscape environment. This line of idea influenced the formulation of the second research question RQ2. RQ 2 sought to investigate the magnitude to which the mountain landscape environment can stimulate human psycho-physiological wellbeing. Hence the question, 'to what degree would the mountain landscape environment influence recovery from directed attention and stress?'. Both directed attention and stress phenomena are determinants of human wellbeing.

Lastly, the third perspective pertains to determination of the aspects of the ambient environment conditions that stimulate human physiological wellbeing. Environmental conditions are precursory ingredients associated with the stress mechanism which serves as a moderator between the environment and human wellbeing (Berto, 2014). A range of physiological responses occur in humans' due to the influence of environmental conditions such as outdoor temperature, atmospheric pressure and relative humidity (Halonen *et al.*, 2011; Okada and Kakehashi, 2014; Werner, 2008). In this case, it was necessary to compare the ambient conditions of the urban environment with that of the mountain landscape environment to ascertain the difference relative to human responses. Thus, RQ 3 concerns the determination of the aspects of the ambient mountain environment conditions which combines to elicit human physiological wellbeing.

The Study Design

This research was approached as a quantitative study. The approach is connected to the psychophysical, experiential and post-positivistic paradigm with which the study was anchored. It supports the use of direct measurements of the psychological and physiological phenomenon of human-environment interaction. Thus, in order to answer the research questions, two research designs were engaged namely: survey and experimental research designs. Table 2.1 shows the relationship between the research questions, design and the sample size.

Table 2.1 Relationship between research questions, design and sample size

STUDY DESIGN: Quantitative (Survey + experimental)			
Questions	**Design**	**Instruments**	**Sample size**
What feature of the mountain landscape environment yields higher restorative benefits in terms of psychological wellbeing?	Cross-sectional survey	Questionnaire	200
What degree would the mountain landscape environment influence recovery from directed attention and stress?	Cross-sectional survey + interrupted time-series within group experimental survey	Questionnaire + physical measurements of physiological indices	38
What aspects of the ambient mountain environment conditions combine to elicit human physiological wellbeing?	Interrupted time-series experimental survey	Instrumented measures with exact calibrations	6 days temperature and humidity data

Survey research design is a quantitative approach which entails administering survey instruments to a sample or population in order to investigate their attitudes, opinions, behaviours or characteristics (Creswell, 2012). In other words, it involves a direct examination of the ways individuals respond to issues pertaining to their attitudes, opinions and beliefs. This study adopted the cross-sectional survey design in dealing with RQ 1. The cross-sectional survey design allows a researcher to select cross-sections of the age span to be studied and enables the examination of developmental transitions over a short period of time (Weathington et al., 2010). It was utilized in order to gain insights into the link between perception of nature and recovery of wellbeing. This was done so as to elicit data on individual's preference and perception of the mountain landscape features in advance of the experimental treatment.

To this end, samples were drawn from a population of urban dwellers, data was collected through a questionnaire and the responses were quantitatively analysed in order to answer RQ 1. RQ 1 queried 'what feature of the mountain landscape environment yields higher restorative benefits in terms of psychological wellbeing?' The reason for engaging samples from the urban environment is because landscape imagined is parallel to an ideal and entails subjective perception expressed in terms of aesthetic and emotional relations (Stoll-Kleemann, 2015).

Both the cross-sectional survey and experimental designs were utilized in investigating the magnitude to which mountain landscape environments stimulate human psychological and physiological well-being. Experimental research design seeks to ascertain and measure the degree to which an intervention (treatment) affect outcome measures either in a laboratory or field research setting (Groat and Wang, 2002). It means that experiments are carried out when the objective of a study is to establish possible cause and effect between variables (Creswell, 2012). This aligns with the context of this study which is the post-positivistic paradigm.

Therefore, to address RQ 2, which queried 'to what degree would the mountain landscape environment influence recovery from directed attention and stress? Accordingly, the within-group experimental design became useful. The within-group experimental design refers to a limited number of individuals studied as a group in an experiment where it is difficult to study more than one group (Creswell, 2012). It is often utilized to examine responses within a single group of individuals whilst comparing human responses in relation to environments. For instance, Lee *et al.*,(2014) and Song *et al.*,(2015a) assessed the influence of forest therapy on human wellbeing using the within-group design. This study utilized the interrupted time series within-group design consisting of only one group studied over a period of time with multiple pre-tests and post-tests by administering intervention measures (Creswell, 2012). Pre-test/post-test designs are primarily used in behavioural research for group comparisons and/or measuring variations arising from experimental treatments (Dimitrov and Rumrill, 2003). In interrupted time series design, data is collected at several points over a period before and after an intervention is introduced to reveal whether it has a significant effect more than the underlying trend (Ramsay *et al.*, 2003).

In this study, the urban environment was used as the pre-test environment while the mountain landscape environment was used as the post-test environment with an interruption in between measures of the group responses. Habitually this method has been used by researchers investigating the restorative potentials of natural environments compared to urban environments (Beil and Hanes, 2013; Hartig *et al.*, 2003; Hartig *et al.*, 1998; Park *et al.*, 2008).

However, psychological and physiological aspects are involved in investigating the extents to which the mountain landscape environment influences recovery from directed attention and stress. Thus, pre-test and post-test measures of psychological responses were carried out using survey questionnaires. This was used to elicit data on the perceived stress of the respondents in the urban environment and their perceived restorativeness in the mountain landscape environment. While physiological responses were carried out through physical measurements of the respondent's physiological indices.

The third research question pertains to the influence of the quality of the ambient environment conditions on human physiological wellbeing. Therefore, the experimental design approach was utilized to compare the ambient urban environment conditions with that of the mountain landscape environment. This involves an exclusively instrumented measure with exact calibration of the instruments (Groat and Wang, 2002). The design also followed the pattern of pre-test, post-test and interrupted time series to acquire data on the ambient environment conditions. In this case, the ambient urban environment constituted the pre-test conditions while the ambient mountain landscape environment constituted the post-test conditions.

Data on the ambient environment conditions were collected concurrently within the same period as the psychological and physiological measures were administered. The essence was to determine if differences exist in ambient environment conditions between the urban and mountain landscape environment and their relationship to physiological wellbeing. This followed the pattern of previous studies investigating the relationship and contribution of ambient environment conditions to the general wellbeing of human beings (Kent *et al.*, 2011; Madsen and Nafstad, 2006; Song *et al.*, 2015a; Tyrväinen *et al.*, 2014).

Parameters of the Study

Following the idea of post-positivism, numeric measures were developed along the line of cause and effect and the study was reduced to specific variables from the questions. It is important to consider the variables in a study in order to identify the items to be measured. The parameters are hereby operationalized in three dimensions as shown in Table 2.2. The dimensions are: (1) preference and perception, (2) psychological and physiological responses, and (3) ambient environment conditions.

Table 2.2 Summary of variables, items of measure and instruments

Dimension/strategy	Variables	Items	Instruments
Preference and perception	• Preference (dependent variable) • Mountain landscape features (independent variables)	Features River, Forest, Built, Water-fall, Mountain vantage point, Artificial water park	Photo questionnaire
	• Perception (dependent variable) • Benefits of contact with the mountain landscape (independent variables)	Benefits Calmness, Stress relief, Excitement, Anxiousness	
Psychological and physiological responses	Psychological • Perceived stress (dependent variable) • Perceived restorativeness (independent variable)	Restorative environment components Being away, Extents, Fascination, Compatibility	Psychological instruments • Perceived stress scale • Perceived restorativeness scale
	Physiological • Directed attention and stress recovery (dependent variable) • Human physiological indices (independent variables)	Indices Blood pressure, Pulse rate, Respiratory rate	Physiological instruments • standard mercury sphygmomanometer • clock with a second hand
Ambient environment conditions	• Ambient environment conditions (predictor independent variables) • Physiological outcomes (dependent variables)	Conditions Temperature, Humidity	Hobo U12 data logger

Preference and Perception

The dimension of preference and perception measured the feature of the mountain landscape environment that yields better restorative benefits in terms of psychological wellbeing. Aesthetic and affective responses are related to visual perceptions of natural environments (Ulrich, 1986). Hence, preference was operationalized as the respondent's inclination for particular features of the mountain landscape environment. Therefore, the variables were preference (as the dependent variable) and the mountain landscape features (as the independent variable) which included river, forest, built structure, waterfall, mountain vantage point and artificial water park.

On the other hand, perception was operationalized as the perceived benefits of contact with the mountain landscape features. Therefore, the variables were perception (as the dependent variable) and the benefits of contact with the mountain landscape features (as the independent variable) which included calmness, relief, excitement and anxiousness. Previous studies have identified calmness, relief, excitement and anxiousness as components of affective responses and positive feelings that determine mental wellbeing (Holbrook, 2009; Scopelliti and Giuliani, 2004; Ulrich, 1986).

Psychological and Physiological Responses

The psychological and physiological dimension of the study measured the degree to which the mountain landscape environment influences recovery from directed attention and stress. Responses to the urban environment which was compared with the mountain landscape environment were measured based on psychological and physiological parameters. The psychological parameters included measures of perceived stress (as the dependent variable) in the urban environment with measures of perceived restoration (as the independent variable) in the mountain landscape environment. The items on the perceived restorativeness scale that were measured are; being away, extent, fascination and compatibility.

The physiological parameters included measures of human physiological indices namely blood pressure, pulse rate and respiratory rate (as measured independent variables). Apart from body temperature, blood pressure, pulse rate and respiratory rate make up a complete set of physiological indices (Cretikos *et al.*, 2008). They are also non-invasive primary measures of stress hence, their choice as variables in this study (McFadden *et al.*, 1982; Sharma and Gedeon, 2012). Recovery from directed attention and stress formed the dependent variables. However, the urban and mountain landscape environments were regarded as the intervening variables. This is based on the cause and effect method employed. Intervening variables are characteristics that influence the dependent variable apart from the independent variable and also mediate the effects of the independent variable on the dependent variable (Creswell, 2012).

Ambient Environment Conditions

The ambient environment conditions dimension is concerned with the aspects of the ambient environment conditions that combine to influence physiological outcome and wellbeing. As such the instrument was designed to measure the ambient conditions of the urban and mountain landscape environment in relation to physiological outcomes in both environments. The ambient environment conditions (as predictor variables) are operationalized as temperature and humidity while the physiological outcomes (as dependent variables) remained blood pressure, pulse rate and respiratory rate.

Unit of Analysis and Sampling Strategy

Urban dwellers were the main unit of assessment in this study. This was based on the context which examined the association between restorative environments, human response and wellbeing. However, the study research design utilized for each question influenced the sampling strategy adopted. Whereas, a single sampling method was utilized, the sample size differed across the research questions.

A non-probability convenience sampling method was deployed in determining the sample for both the survey and experimental aspects. Because of the experimental nature of the study and following the idea of Creswell (2012), only individuals who volunteer and agreed to be studied made up the sample. A few of the volunteers who were known acquaintances at the Benue State University, Nigeria were initially co-opted by the researcher. These initial volunteers then co-opted others to make up the sample. Also, individual's behaviour was a determinant in the selection of volunteers (Weathington *et al.*, 2010) who eventually constituted the sample for the experiment. But only individuals who were non-smokers (Lee *et al.*, 2013), not on any form of cardiovascular related drug and not at the time of experimentation suffering from any acute illnesses were selected (Abdulla and Taka, 1988). This process was done through verbal questioning (Okada and Kakehashi, 2014).

According to Onwuegbuzie and Collins (2007), the sample size in an investigation should be informed primarily by the research objectives, questions and designs. The study sample which relates to the cross-sectional survey and pertains to preference and perception involved 200 respondents drawn from a population of lecturers and students of the Benue State University, Makurdi, Nigeria. This category of respondents was selected because of their educational level and capacity to understand questions. The number was arrived at after 250 questionnaires were distributed to respondents and 202 were returned with 2 declared invalid due to multiple entries. Based on the size needed for statistical procedures, Creswell (2012) suggests that 350 individuals are adequate for a survey study depending on several other factors. The non-probability convenience sampling method employed influenced the sample size of 200. However, previous studies on environmental preferences and perception have demonstrated that the sample size of 138 (Herzog and

Shier, 2000), 170 (Herzog and Kropscott, 2004) and 202 (Lindemann-Matthies *et al.*, 2010) were enough to derive significant conclusions. The demographics of respondents revealed that 137 of the total number were males while 63 were females. All respondents were between the ages of 21 to 50 years old.

The study sample relating to the cross-sectional and experimental survey pertains to Question 2. It concerns the aspect dealing with the psychological and physiological responses of respondents in the urban and mountain landscape environments. Forty respondents comprising lecturers, students and public-sector workers between the ages of 20 to 40 years were recruited from the urban environment of Makurdi, Benue State, Nigeria. This forty were not part of the 200 respondents used in the cross-sectional survey dealing with preference and perception. A day before the experiment commenced, two of the respondents opted out. One due to the time factor and the other admitted not being psychologically stable for the experiments. Thirty-eight respondents including 16 males and 22 females between the ages of 20 and 40 years old gave informed written consent to participate in the study. All the thirty-eight respondents formed a within group experimental study, while the third objective which entailed measures of the ambient environment conditions did not require sampling. It was linked with the second objective which concerns the psychological and physiological responses.

Study Locations; Urban and Mountain Landscape Environment

In studies relating to stress and restorative potential of environments, the main distinguishing factor of the environments were the physical characteristics (Berman *et al.*, 2008; Brown *et al.*, 2013; van den Berg *et al.*, 2014). This study involved the comparison between urban and mountain landscape environment.

Makurdi urban environment is the capital city of Benue State, Nigeria was used as the pre-test environment. Its choice as a study location was due to its urban character and also related to the non-probability convenience sampling method. Figure 2.2 show photos of Makurdi urban environment setting. It has a tropical savanna climate with an annual average temperature range between 32.6°C and 21.8°C. Makurdi comprises of urban attributes of hardscapes, population density, commercial activities and heavy traffic that lies on an altitude of about 104m above sea level. The aforementioned characteristics constitute sources of stress for individuals.

Figure 2.2 Makurdi urban environment setting

The post-test environment was the Obudu mountains in Obanliku local government area of Cross River State, Nigeria. It has a semi-temperate mountain climate and an altitude ranging between 1700m and 1765m above sea level. During the dry season of November to January, temperature ranges between 26°C and 32°C. The rainy season starting from June to October is colder with temperatures as low as 4°C and usually not higher than 10°C. Temperatures between February and May fluctuate between night time when it is usually low and daytime when it is mostly high. It is characterized by diverse landscape attributes such as waterfall, grotto, river, forest reserve, 70m long canopy walkway, bird watching platform, cable car ride. The cable car ride affords a motion view of prominent undulating mountain formations covered by near dense but fascinating green vegetation. Hence, the environment offers serene ambience suitable for stress mitigation. Some of these features illustrated in Figure 2.3 show photos of the Obudu mountain landscape environment character.

Figure 2.3 Some attributes and features of Obudu mountain landscape environment

(**A**-river feature, **B**-mountain vantage point, **C**-canopy walkway, **D**-waterfall, **E**-built structures, **F**-Water theme park, **G**-view from the cable car, **H**-the cable cars)

Information Extraction Process

Data extraction allows a researcher to record and quantify observations objectively and consistently (Weathington *et al.*, 2010). It is an important means of providing answers to research questions. Psychological and physiological data were collected through attitudinal measures and experimental observations. The attitudinal measures involved emotional scales that measured positive or negative responses given by respondents towards the environment (Creswell, 2012). Conversely, the experimental observations involved physical measurements and record of respondent's physiological indices and ambient environment conditions.

Preference and Perception of the Mountain Landscape Features

A questionnaire was developed and modified to measure the variables pertaining to respondent's preference and perception of the mountain landscape features. It was developed and modified following examples and methods adopted by previous studies (Bulut *et al.*, 2010; Galindo and Hidalgo, 2005; Pazhouhanfar and Kamal, 2014; Uduma-Olugu, 2013). Before the survey, the questionnaire was discussed with experts in landscape architecture and perception studies (Lindemann-Matthies *et al.*, 2010). The critique that emerged from the discussion led to the modification of the questionnaire by removing confusing issues. The standardized 3-page questionnaire contains texts and 6 colour photographs with a scale attached to the top photographs embedded in a single frame. All the photographs were oriented horizontally on the frame in one page to allow the respondents to view all images simultaneously.

These 6 photographs each representing a specific feature of the mountain landscape environment was selected from 30 photographs captured in specific locations in the Obudu mountain landscape environment. Only 6 photographs were selected to avoid confusing the respondents, who were largely non-experts in the area of landscape assessment (Hidalgo *et al.*, 2006). Photos have been found to be valid in so far as the intent of evaluations is based on the information in the photo (Scott and Canter, 1997). Also, Wilkie and Stavridou (2013) are in support of the appropriateness of using imagery to understand an individual's judgement of the restorative potential of an environment. The rationale for using this process is supported by the study conducted by Schirpke *et al.*, (2013a) in which a photographic questionnaire depicting diverse alpine landscapes was utilized. Clarity and quality of the photos determined their selection. To ensure the clarity and quality of the photos, the camera is held at eye level and focused on a horizontal plane when photos are taken (Snyder and Allen, 1975). The photographs were taken at midday to avoid the characteristic misty weather of Obudu mountain landscape environment in August during the pilot study prior to the main research. The photos depicted six major features of the Obudu mountain landscape environment namely: river, forest, built structures, waterfall, mountain vantage point and artificial water park. Each photograph was labelled by text according to the character of the feature.

The questionnaire was made up of four sections (See Appendix A). Section A elicited data on the demographics of respondents including gender, age, marital status, nationality and occupation. Section B required the respondents to rate the photographs depicting scenes of the features of the mountain landscape environment in order of preference. This was to identify the feature of the mountain landscape environment that yield restorative benefits in terms of psychological wellbeing. Because of the quantitative method adopted, an ordinal scale which is rank ordered was used (Weathington *et al.*, 2010). Specifically, the ratings were on a 5-point Likert scale (1= not preferred; 5=highly preferred). The respondents were instructed to write any of the numbers on the scale representing the range which captures their opinion in a box at the corner of each photograph. Section C involved two parts. The first part required the respondents to indicate on a list of the same features projected as photographs in Section B whether they have had contact with any or more of the features. The questionnaire instructed respondents to tick one or more of the features that conform to the aforementioned. The options on the list were river, forest, built structures, waterfall, mountain vantage point and artificial water park features as in the photographs in Section B.

However, the second part of Section C required the response of the participants in terms of their perceived benefit of contact with the mountain landscape features. This is in order to elicit the participants' perception of the contribution of the mountain landscape features to human wellbeing. This is based on the assertion of Bell *et al.*, (2001) that perceptual responses can be acquired through predictions of the contributions of a particular physical ingredient of a scene with regards to its perceived value. The respondents were asked to score calmness, relief, anxiousness and excitement on a 5-point Likert scale ranging from strongly disagree (1) to strongly agree (5). The question specifically asked 'What do you perceive to be the benefit of your contact with the landscape features shown in Section B?' They were instructed to circle a number that reflects their perception based on the scale.

The questionnaires were distributed to the respondents by five assistants from the Benue State University Makurdi, Nigeria and the researcher on a face to face basis. Prior to the distribution, research assistants were properly briefed on etiquettes and manner of engaging respondents. For instance, they have to reassure the respondents of the confidentiality of their responses and also not to be rude when turned down by potential respondents. In other words, anonymity was guaranteed to the respondents. At the end 200 valid questionnaire forms were used for analysis.

Experimentation of the Psycho-physiological Responses

This section pertains to the instruments and procedures involved in data extraction to answer research question Q2 which sought to investigate the magnitude to which the mountain landscape environment can stimulate human psychophysiological wellbeing. The instruments and procedures were used to extract data concerning the degree to which the mountain landscape environment would influence recovery from directed attention and stress. Data were extracted in two stages and two places, the pre-test and post-test environments. This involved two aspects, psychological and physiological responses of respondents in both environments. In retrospect, the pre-test environment was the urban environment while the post-test environment was the mountain landscape environment. Accordingly, this is explained under two headings, the psychological measures which involved survey questionnaires and the physiological measures which involved experimentation.

Psychological Measures

To ascertain the psychological wellbeing of the respondents, their perceived stress in the urban environment and perceived restorativeness in the mountain landscape environment was measured. These involved obtaining subjective psychological responses of respondents using scaled questionnaires namely; perceived stress scale (Cohen *et al.*, 1983) and perceived restorativeness scale (Hartig *et al.*, 1997). The perceived stress scale (PSS) and perceived restorativeness scale (PRS) questionnaires are valid scales used in studies to investigate psychological human responses to environmental stimuli (Andreou *et al.*, 2011; Beil and Hanes, 2013; Berto, 2007).

The perceived stress of the respondents was evaluated based on a 13 items version of the perceived stress scale. The 13 items version was arrived at after the revision of the constructs of the 14 questions version of Cohen *et al.* (1983). This revision was based on the outcome of the exploratory study. A final version based on 13 items was administered on the respondents. Respondents scored the 13 items based on a 5-point Likert scale (1= never; 5=very often) to specify their feelings and thoughts in the urban environment. The questionnaire was administered on the 38 respondents in the urban environment (pre-test) before the intervention in the mountain landscape environment (post-test). Since the 38 respondents also formed the within group experimental study, the questionnaire forms were filled and returned immediately.

In order to measure psychological responses as it pertains to the experience of restoration, all the 38 respondents also completed the perceived restorativeness scale (PRS). The PRS version of Hartig *et al.* (1997) consisting four set of the attention restoration components describe the being away, extent, fascination and compatibility variables. The variables in this version contain different sets of items (being away-6, extent-5, fascination-6, compatibility-7) totalling 24. However, this version was also modified based on the outcome of the exploratory study. On the basis of the reliability analysis, items that caused low consistency rating on the extent and fascination components were removed (Hartig *et al.*, 1996). Specifically, the item '*this environment makes me feel like am in a larger setting*' in the extent construct was removed. Also, the item '*this environment has many things that I wonder about*' in the fascination construct was removed. With the removal of these items, the final version of the PRS administered contained 22 questions.

Respondents scored items of the four variables on a 5-point rating scale (1= strongly disagree; 5= strongly agree) based on their experience of the mountain landscape environment. This questionnaire was administered on the third day of intervention at the mountain environment to ensure that subject's psychological responses were fully obtained.

Physiological Measures

The experimentation was carried out between 28th January and 3rd February 2014. The experimental protocol spanned 7 days as shown in Figure 2.4. Pre-test measures were carried out at the urban environment on 28th, 29th and 30th January which represent first three days of the study. Post-test measures were carried out at the mountain landscape environment the following three days, 1st, 2nd and 3rd February. Three qualified medics assisted in carrying out measurements at the urban environment while two assisted at the mountain landscape environment. The respondents were verbally briefed at the beginning of the study on the measures to be taken which included systolic blood pressure, diastolic blood pressure, pulse rate and respiratory rate measurements. This briefing was done in order to alleviate fear and anxiety of the respondents concerning the procedure (O'Brien *et al.*, 2003).

The pre-test centre for the measurements was set at the Benue State University Makurdi medical school's private dining hall which was within a 10-km radius and about fifteen-minute drive from the location of each respondent. Measurements were carried out between 6 pm and 8 pm during the three-day period at the urban environment. Each respondent was allowed to rest in a seated position on arrival at the pre-test centre for at least five minutes before their blood pressure (BP), pulse rate and respiratory rate were taken. Respondents were asked to put off their phones to avoid distraction and disturbance. Systolic blood pressure (BP), diastolic blood pressure (BP), pulse rate and respiratory rate of each respondent were recorded for the three consecutive days.

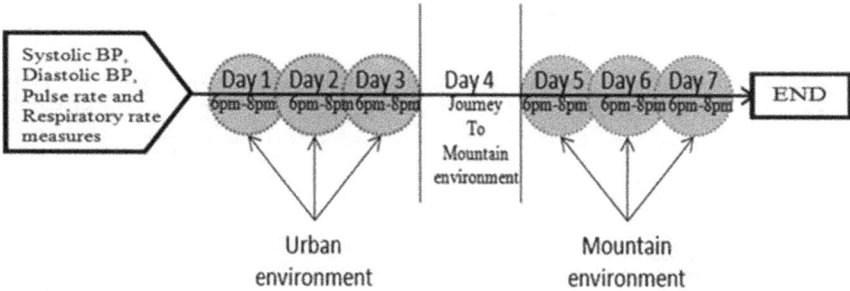

Figure 2.4 The 7 days experimental protocol showing measurement time

Respondents were transported by road on a journey that lasted 4 hours to the Obudu mountain landscape environment on the 31st of January 2014. They were allowed to take a rest and interact freely on arrival, but measurements were not taken that day in order to check the effect of 'travel fatigue' (Waterhouse *et al.*, 2004). Systolic BP, diastolic BP, pulse rate and respiratory rates were carried out every day throughout the three-day period at the mountain landscape environment using the same equipment and process as obtained in the urban environment. Similar to the procedure in the urban environment, measures were carried out between 6pm and 8pm each day. This was to ensure that respondents had had considerable contact with features of the Mountain landscape environment which included a waterfall, river, forest and visual experience of the undulating mountains before measures were taken. The pre-test and post-test measures were also carried out within the same time frame (6pm to 8pm) in order to check the influence of circadian effect (Biaggioni, 2008; Ochiai *et al.*, 2015).

Blood pressure measurement was performed by the medics using the standard mercury sphygmomanometer and the auscultatory technique. This technique is dependent on the accurate transmission and interpretation of a signal (Korotkoff sound) from an individual through the sphygmomanometer to the medic (O'Brien *et al.*, 2003). This involved the use of a stethoscope held over the artery just below the cuff by the medic to listen and detect the sounds (Pickering *et al.*, 2005). Figure 2.5 shows the standard mercury sphygmomanometers and stethoscope. The standard mercury sphygmomanometers used in this study were properly checked and found to be free of leakages to ensure the accuracy of measurements (De Greeff *et al.*, 2010). Its simplicity and lack of major difference between models makes it more accurate than other types of manometers hence, its choice as the blood pressure measuring device (Pickering *et al.*, 2005). The outcome of previous studies that examined relationships between blood pressure and human wellbeing also confirms its validity (Abdulla and Taka, 1988; Chen *et al.*, 2013; Marazziti *et al.*, 1992).

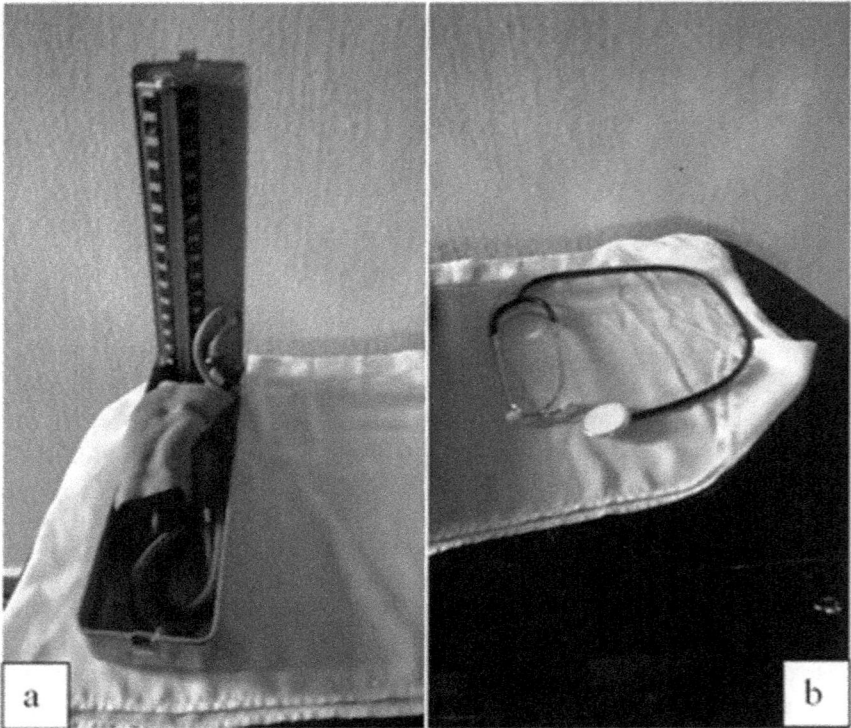

Figure 2.5 The standard mercury sphygmomanometer (a) and stethoscope (b)

To reduce possible errors in measurements and obtain a valid and reliable blood pressure data, the procedure followed recommendations of O'Brien *et al.* (2003) and Pickering *et al.* (2005) on blood pressure measurement outlined below. Also, Figure 2.6 shows the procedure being performed on some respondents in the pre-test and post-test environment.

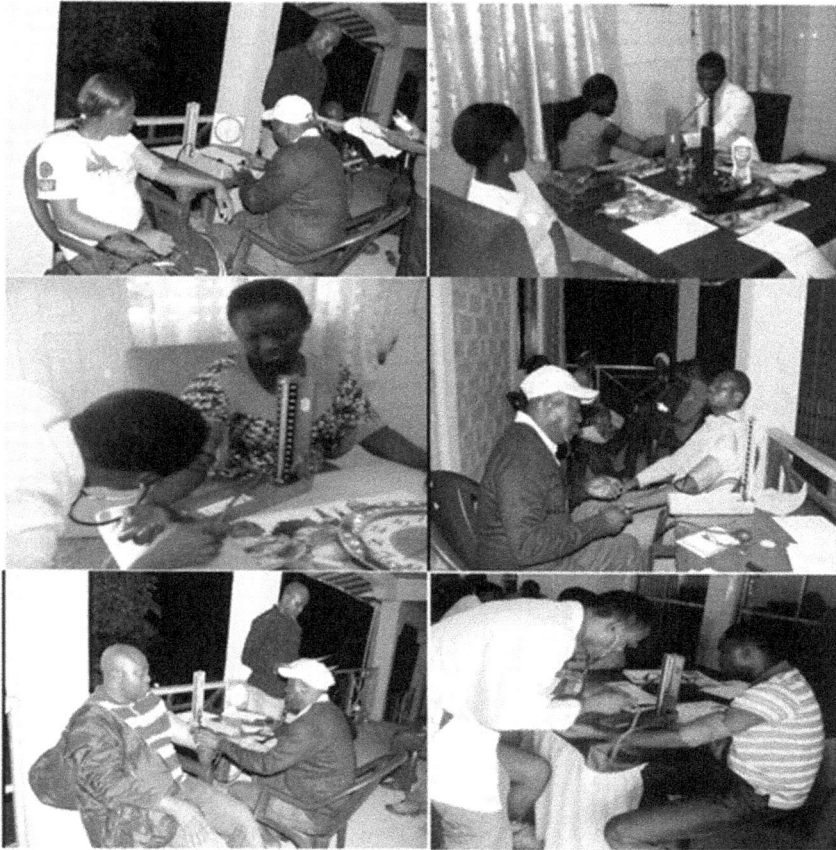

Figure 2.6 The procedure being performed on some respondents

I. All the medics were properly briefed on the research protocol to ensure similar steps and techniques.

II. Adequate explanation was made to the respondents regarding the procedure in order to ease their fear and anxiety.

III. A short period of rest of about 5 minutes preceding measurement was observed and it was carried out in a quiet environment at a comfortable temperature. In the pre-test environment, it was carried out in a quiet room without artificial air condition but good ventilation. In the post-test environment, it was carried out outdoors but also in a very quiet location.

IV.   Respondents were made to be in a seating position with the arm supported at the heart level, feet firmly on the floor and back supported by chair.

V.   Cuffs were long enough to encircle the arm of an adult several times in a suitable and appropriate way. Clothing around the arm where the cuff would be encircled was exposed.

VI.   The readings were recorded in a table provided on a piece of paper with columns for all the physiological indices measured.

The process of measuring pulse rate involved the use of a clock with a functional second hand. Respondents' pulse which is the throbbing of the artery signifying the rate of heartbeats and flow of blood through the body was felt at the wrist (Figure 2.7). This was done by the medics following the right clinical procedures.

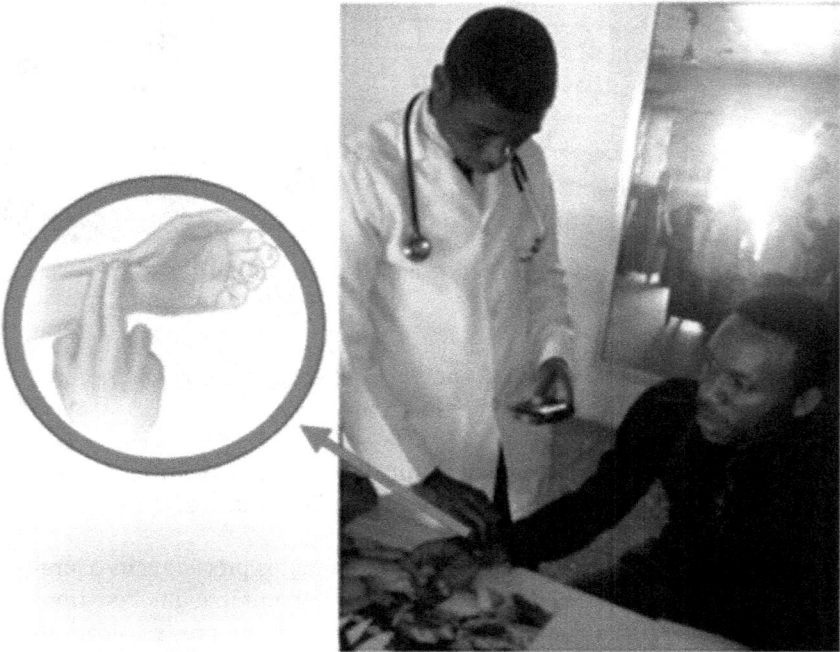

Figure 2.7 The pulse rate procedure being performed on a respondent

The pulse rate of all respondents was also recorded on the record sheet provided. Recording respiratory rate involves observation of the respiratory circle which is made up of an inhalation and exhalation period (Plarre *et al.*, 2011). The pattern of respiration was visually counted on the basis of the 60 seconds count method (Cretikos *et al.*, 2008). This process was carried out in a way that the respondent being observed was unaware their respiration was being observed (McFadden *et al.*, 1982). This was to ensure that respondents do not manipulate their breaths. The range of breaths per minute was then recorded on the record sheet by the medics. The pulse rate and respiratory rate measurements immediately followed the blood pressure measurement in a consecutive pattern.

Measures of the Ambient Environment Conditions

This part explains the instruments and procedures used in data collection pertaining to the ambient environment conditions. It sought to determine the effect of temperature and humidity on physiological wellbeing. To provide real time measurement of temperature and humidity the 'onset hobo U12 model' data logger was used (Figure2.8).

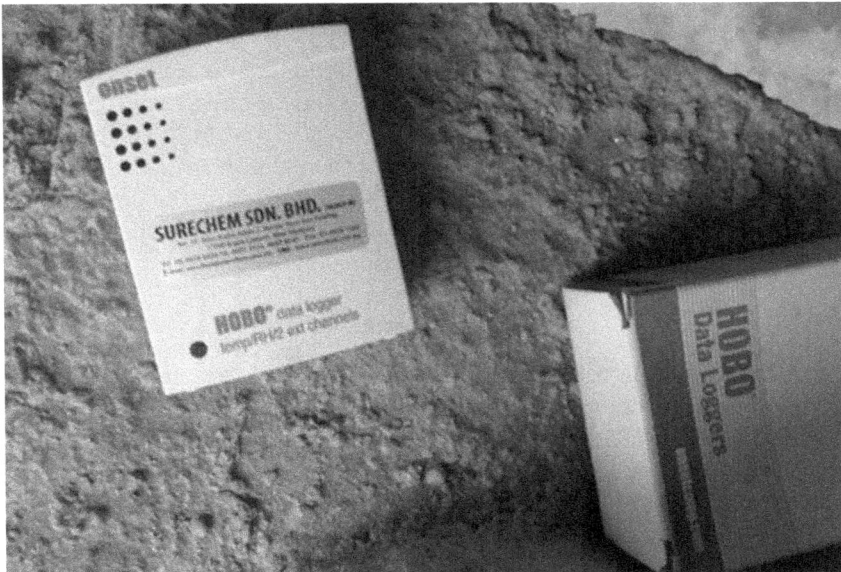

Figure 2.8 The onset hobo U12 data logger

The data logger is a computerized electronic device that measures and records periodic environment conditions in real time. Its real-time collection and presentation of data with sensors that are able to respond to parameters beyond the normal range makes the data logger an invaluable instrument for experimental data collection and analysis (Waghmare and Chatur, 2012).

The temperature and humidity data extraction took place during the same period as the physiological indices of respondents were being taken both in the urban and mountain environments. The device was set-up and launched in the pre-test environment a day before commencement of physiological indices measures. This was to ensure that the correct range of data was recorded. It was placed in 4-inches polyvinyl chloride (PVC) pipe section wrapped with aluminium foil and fixed outdoors under a building roof eave to protect it from direct contact with any kind of fluid. It recorded series of real-time temperature and humidity data for 84 hours but only data for 72 hours during the experimental period of 28th to 30th January, 2014 was utilized for analysis. On the day of the journey to the mountain landscape environment, the device was removed from its position and recording stopped. On arrival at the mountain landscape environment on the 31st of January 2014 the device was re-launched. It was also fixed outdoors following the same method employed in the urban environment. The device recording was stopped on conclusion of physiological measures at the mountain landscape environment.

This set of data captured the three-day experimental period in the urban environment and similarly in the mountain environment with one-hour intervals between measurements (Jamaludin *et al.*, 2013). A single unit of data logger was used in recording data in both environments. The temperature and humidity data were eventually downloaded from the device into a personal computer for data analysis. Data which did not fall within the experimental days were excluded.

Analysis of the Extracted data

The data collected through the three measurements strategies were analysed using statistical package for the social sciences (SPSS version 19) software. The analysis carried out included descriptive and inferential statistics across the measurement strategies. In Strategy 1 which pertains to preference and perception of respondents in relation to the mountain landscape environment features, descriptive statistics such as simple percentages and mean scores were adopted.

Conversely, analysis of variance (ANOVA) test was performed to determine whether significant differences exist among the groups. The ANOVA test is adopted when there are more than two groups to be considered. Thus, it was adopted to test how the different age categories differ in their perceived preference and perception of the benefits of the mountain landscape features. In contrast, t-test is adopted when only two groups are involved and, in this study, it was used in testing gender differences in response to perceived preference of mountain landscape features.

In Strategy 2 which involved respondent's psychological and physiological responses in relation to pre-test and post-test measures, the data obtained where analysed through inferential statistics. Specifically, regression analysis was performed. This was done to determine the effect of the PRS constructs (Being away, Extent, Fascination, and Compatibility) on perceived stress. Physiological responses were analysed using the paired sample t-test to determine whether the effect of contact with the pre-test and post-test environments differ. Furthermore, a one-way analysis of variance (ANOVA) test was performed to ascertain the difference in systolic blood pressure, diastolic blood pressure, pulse rate and respiratory rate responses based on age groups.

Lastly, data which concerns the determination of the effect of the difference in ambient environment conditions on wellbeing were analysed using the t-test and multiple linear regression analysis. T-test was used to ascertain the effect of differences in temperature and humidity between the pre-test and post-test environments. Multiple linear regression analysis was employed to determine the contribution and association of temperature and humidity to changes in systolic, diastolic BP, pulse rate and respiratory rate.

Validity and Reliability Assessment

The idea of validity and reliability pertains to the degree to which an instrument evidently measures what it is actually meant to measure (Sitiza, 2009). In terms of validity, a valid test refers to the situation where a researcher using an instrument tends to make accurate conclusions based on test scores or responses (Weathington *et al.*, 2010). The validity of the study was underpinned by the measurements, instruments and methods employed in exploring the restorative benefits of contact with the mountain landscape environment. Thus, the following strategies were employed in order to ensure validity:

I.   Ensuring that all respondents have equal chance of exposure to the experimental conditions led to a clear causal inference (Bell *et al.*, 2001). This was achieved through the within group experimental design. The same group of respondents that received the pre-test treatment in the urban environment received the post-test treatment in the mountain landscape environment. This ensured that true difference in comparison between the two environments which may be masked by the presence of extraneous factors was guaranteed (Daniel and Cross, 2010). For instance, physiological measures were not carried out on the day respondents were transported to the mountain landscape environment in order to prevent the effect of 'travel fatigue'. Therefore, the cause and effect dimensions of environmental stimuli on directed attention and stress were adequately explored.

II.   Data were acquired through measures of the variables related to the theories that underpinned this study (Mitchell and Jolley, 2012). The constructs of attention restoration theory and stress restorative theory were examined through the combination of psychological and physiological measures. This was different from previous methods employed by researchers examining the constructs of the aforementioned theories. Hence, the results obtained which concur with the underlying constructs of the theories establish its validity (Bell *et al.*, 2001).

III.   Studies pertaining to environments done in quasi settings lack the realism associated with natural environments. Real site studies provide far reaching evidence than indoor studies as regards environments (Lee *et al.*, 2012). Therefore, the real site and mountain landscape environment situatedness also enhanced the validity of this study. This means that the study has a lot of ecological value, thus it can be generalized to other natural environment settings (Mitchell and Jolley, 2012).

Reliability refers to the consistency of observations and measurements (Weathington *et al.*, 2010) or the accuracy of an instrument (Heale and Twycross, 2015). A multi-dimensional approach was used in the measurements and observations carried out. In other words, multiple instruments and measurement procedures were engaged. Thus, reliability was estimated based on each instrument and the observed dimension.

The relationship between validity and reliability involves the convergence of measures and results obtained on the constructs of the study. However, no test is perfectly valid and reliable due to random events that can heighten or lower the responses on a given instrument (Weathington *et al.*, 2010). Therefore, to enhance the validity and reliability of results, different types of data were collected with different types of instruments (Zohrabi, 2013). In other words, data triangulation was employed. To this end, the three-approach utilized in collecting data towards answering the three research questions provided results that were interwoven.

Synthesis of Findings from the Study Constructs

This study focused on the assumption that nature offers restorative qualities and the exploration of the link between mountain landscape environments, human response and wellbeing. It sought to know the features responsible for wellbeing, the extents of recovery and the ambient conditions acting on the restoration of directed attention and stress mitigation in the mountain landscape environment.

Therefore, this section conveys the conclusion from the synthesis of results and findings of the study hence, parallels and differences were highlighted while anticipated and surprising outcomes were emphasized. It is structured into two key aspects. Firstly, evidence of human perception and psychological response is highlighted. Secondly, evidence of experiential psychological and physiological wellbeing is accentuated.

Evidence of human Perception and Psychological Response

The perception and psychological responses of individuals to the mountain landscape features was demonstrated in this study through subjective evaluation which yielded cognitive and perceptual evidence. This aspect of the study explored the cognitive and perceptual assessment of features of the mountain landscape environment by individuals through preference judgments of surrogate photos. The study was able to identify which aspect of the mountain landscape environment potentially influence human perception through preference and perceived restorative benefits. As shown in Figure 2.9, it was found that artificial water park received the highest preference rating while the river and forest features received the least. The study, however, anticipated that individuals would prefer the non-structured (like the river and forest) rather than human structured (like the artificial water park) features of the mountain landscape environment. This expectation is leveraged on researchers' assertion that human preference for different landscapes or the perception of aesthetic qualities of any landscape depends on human knowledge and understanding which may be innate, learned or procured. In this instance, the findings suggest that though human preference for a particular feature of the environment is the product of knowledge and understanding it cannot be said to be innate given that the feature was not experienced but perceived through surrogates. This research, therefore, concludes that cultural bias due to familiarity of the individuals with the structured features and not innate human characteristics is responsible for their preference. This is inconsistent with the speculations of evolutionary perspective.

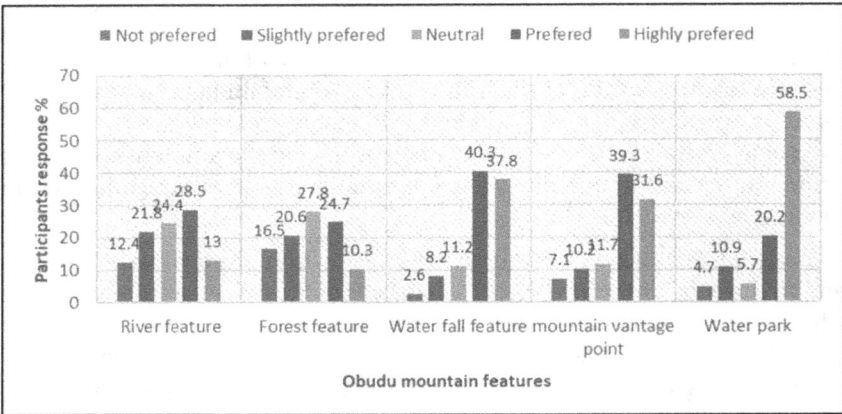

Figure 2.9 Overall preference rating for the mountain environment features

Whilst this study did not anticipate differences in preference of the features between age groups, the pattern of ratings in that regard revealed mixed findings showing diverse degrees of preference for the mountain landscape features. Figure 2.10 shows the preference levels of individuals for the features across the age groups. Individuals are likely to relate with mountain landscape environment features based on a certain phenomenon which have been identified by this study to modify preference depending on the age group. It was found that young adults (31 – 40 years old) and adults (41 – 50 years old) preferred the river and forest feature more than the young (21 – 30 years old). This means that perception is enhanced by the modifying factor of meaning giving to a particular landscape feature from memory of past encounter which could be generational due to urban growth. Most urban areas were hitherto hinterlands with forests and river features. However, human activities due to urban growth depleted these natural resources giving way to more man-made resources. Hence, only the generation that encountered the natural state of the environment are able to identify its features and allocate meanings. The finding supports the assertions that people who are less familiar with landscape types have difficulty reading and allocating meaning to landscapes because landscape variety in urban environments has decreased (Kaplan and Kaplan, 1989).

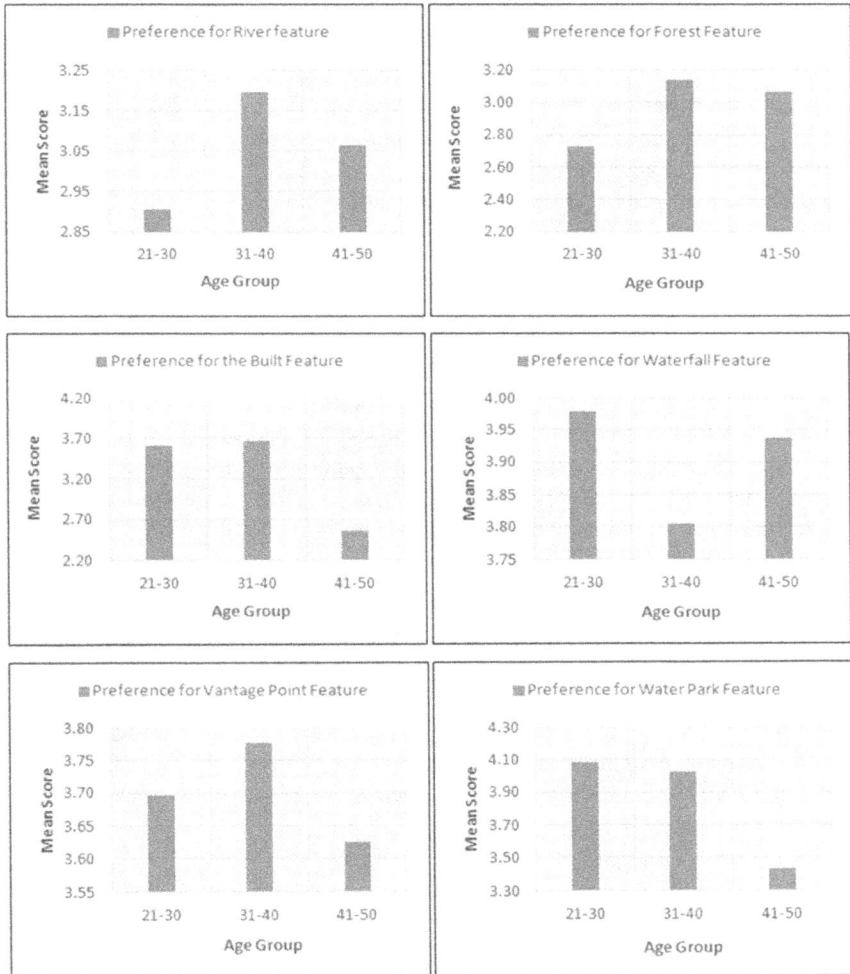

Figure 2.10 Preference level for the features across age groups

Young individuals (21 – 30 years old) and young adults (31 – 40 years old) preferred the built feature more than the adults (41 – 50 years old). This finding is consistent with the concept of the components of an environment in terms of compatibility (Chang *et al.*, 2008). The built and natural features mixed together influenced individual variations in preference due to compatibility. As such young individuals and young adults perceived the features in terms of personal preference, the presence of the platform for desired activities and action. Another modifier of preference in terms of age that was found involves the perceived stimulation likelihood of the mountain landscape features. Young individuals were found to prefer the waterfall feature more than young adults and adults. This was unexpected and indicates that individuals react to different types of water bodies in diverse ways based on the finding that young adults and adults preferred the river feature more than the young individuals. Hence, young adults and adults prefer hard rather than soft stimulants of the mountain landscape environment which further supports the idea of this study that as individuals age their affinity for the thrilling aspects of nature reduces.

The next modifier of preference for landscape features that was found involves the environment and the features in it. It was found that adults were neutral in their preference rating of the mountain landscape vantage point, whereas the young and young adults prefer artificial water park feature more than adults. Apart from showing that the familiarity phenomenon is shared across the age groups, individuals are likely to access landscape based on its content not the container, despite the possibilities in having access to long views from the mountain vantage point. This finding is unexpected and inconsistent with studies supporting the influence of distant zones on human recognition and understanding of landscape (Miller, 2001; Schirpke *et al.*, 2013a).

With regards to gender, difference occurred between male and female in their preferences for the mountain landscape features, but the modifiers of their perception were not investigated. This finding is, however, in accord with studies demonstrating gender differences for specific landscape stimuli. In sum, the extent of human influence and presence of water forms the most important aspects of landscape perception. Therefore, be it mountain or lowland, the object of preference will be what is contained in the environment and not the environment itself.

Cognitive and Perceptual Evidence of Restorative Benefits

Aesthetic and affective responses are linked to visual perceptions of the natural environment. Apart from aesthetic values, the mountain landscape features were also perceived as having restorative benefits in terms of affective values. This speculation gained support from the findings of this study which suggests that excitement, calmness and stress relief are the most benefits that can be derived from the mountain landscape environment. Although the perception of the individual was based on subjective judgements, the finding suggests that individuals are prone to experience feelings of excitement when they physically interact with nature. Calmness and relief are positive feelings generated by the individual's fascination instigated through visuals of natural environments. The mountain landscape environment is not an exception in this regard. From a theoretical point of view, fascination implies that individual's feelings are captured by particular stimuli (Kaplan, 1995). Therefore, the high preference ratings of water features (artificial water park and waterfall) by the individuals in this study cannot be ignored. Given this evidence, it is therefore adequate to say that water features contribute greatly to the perception of the mountain landscape as a fascinating environment capable of restoration of stress.

On the other hand, only anxiousness was perceived as not being a part of the restorative benefit of the mountain landscape features. Therefore, plant, water, and other natural features present in the mountain landscape environment would be unable to mitigate anxiety. This is inconsistent with studies suggesting that contact with nature scenes have a mitigating influence on the individual's anxiety states (Bratman *et al.*, 2015; Ulrich, 1979). Hence, with regards to perception, mountain landscape environments are unlikely to influence the stress response system by way of alleviating anxiety. Interestingly, anxiousness was not perceived as a benefit of interacting with the mountain landscape features across the age groups.

Regarding the perception of calmness, relief and excitement as benefits of interaction with the mountain landscape features, the response and findings across the age groups were diverse. It was found that the young and young adults agreed more than the adults to the notion that mountain landscape features offer restorative benefits in terms of calmness, relief and excitement. Therefore, perception of restorative potential of the mountain landscape environment varies across age groups. Contextual factors accounted mainly for these variations in three dimensions.

Firstly, the finding across the age groups is evidence that implies that individuals are likely to underrate the benefits of nature. From the methodology employed by this study to achieve Objective 1 with regards to the perception of the mountain landscape features as being restorative, photos were utilized. Hence, an individual's capacity to imagine the scenes and perceive its benefits is relied upon. Therefore, this study establishes that young and young adults value the mountain landscape environment more than adults in terms of calmness. Also, preference for certain landscape features does not indicate high judgements of restoration potential. Based on the findings, young and young adults preferred the built and structured landscape features more than the adults. This is not in support of the assertion of Wilkie and Stavridou (2013) which suggests that high restorative potential ratings would be anticipated for images in agreement with the environment that is more preferred rather than those not in agreement. Therefore, the built and structured environments features such as those found in urban environments are not meant to generate restorative potential rather they are likely to form part of stressors. Hence, the young and young adults who preferred the built and structured features comparably perceived the mountain landscape features as a whole to be beneficial in terms of calmness more than the adults.

Secondly, all through the life circle of an individual, perception changes with a change in context and experience leading to the suggestion that genetic makeup and evolutionary history is not the reason for the love for nature. This emanates from the fact that, young and young adults agreed while adults disagreed that stress relief was a potential benefit of interaction with the mountain landscape environment. This is in addition to the conclusion that cultural bias and not innate human characteristics influence individual preference. Also, different age groups react differently to the perception of restoration in environments. The young and young adults perceived the mountain landscape environment features as being beneficial in terms of relief because they anticipated that their restorative goals would be met while the adults did not. Therefore, it differs from the claim that humans, due to their genetic makeup and evolutionary history, generally feel an innate love for natural environments (Kellert, 1995; Wilson, 1984). However, this finding supports 'being away', one of the components of a restorative environment prescribed in attention restoration theory which entails the perception of the physical environment and activities within it as being different.

Thirdly, similar to the outcome of the perception of age groups in terms of relief, it was found that young and young adults agreed while adults disagreed that excitement was part of the benefits of interacting with the mountain landscape features. The type and time of exposure required before excitement could be generated in an environment is important in considering the reason for the variance in perception of the age groups. The type of exposure, in this case, was through questionnaire photos while the time of exposure was brief. It implies that the young and young adults psychologically perceived the mountain landscape features as an environment capable of generating excitement better than the adults. Although the available literature on the relationship between excitement and the restorative potential of an environment is slim, given a real site situation and adequate time the young and young adults will feel more excitement than the adults. It means that excitement increases especially among young individuals with available time for restoration.

Asides these contextual factors that accounted for variations in the perception of the mountain landscape features restorative benefits across the age groups, no gender difference occurred. This shows that perception of the restorative benefits of the mountain landscape features has no bearing on gender.

Figure 2.11 shows a thematic sketch of the evidence of human perception and psychological response to the mountain landscape features. Through cognition and perception, the artificial water park is the most preferred while river and forest features were the least preferred features. The reason is due to cultural bias stemming from familiarity and not innate characteristics. The modifying factors of preference across the age groups were identified as meaning, compatibility, hard and soft stimulants and content not container. The restorative bene-fits in terms of affective values of the mountain landscape features are excite-ment, calmness and relief whereas anxiousness was perceived as not beneficial.

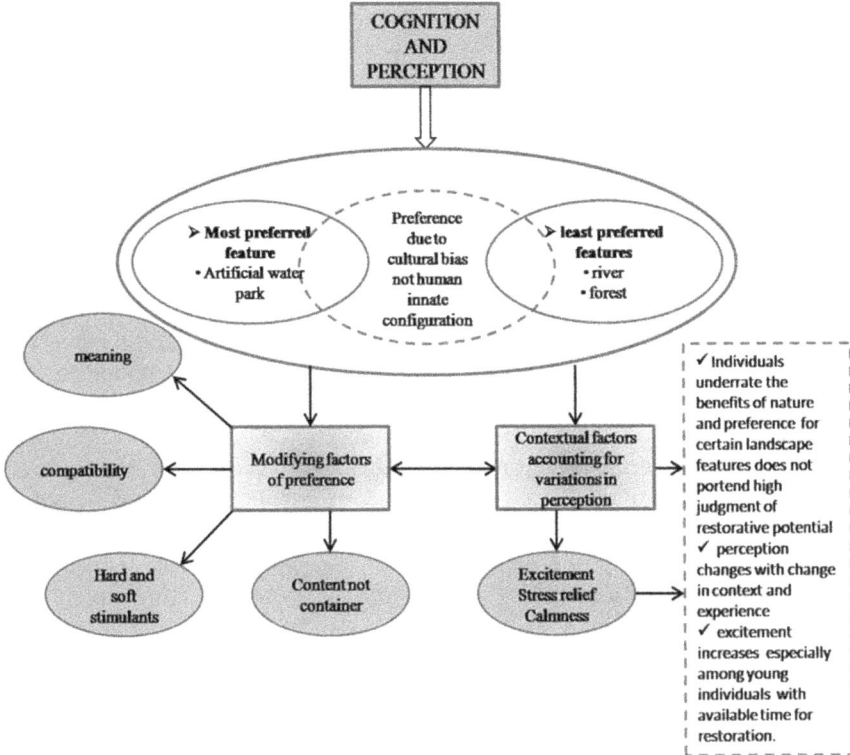

Figure 2.11 Evidence of Perception and Psychological response

Evidence of Experiential Psychological and Physiological Wellbeing

Psychological and physiological evidence of wellbeing were acquired in this study which involved physical contact and experience of both the urban and mountain environments comparatively. The evidence revealed the magnitude to which mountain landscape environments can stimulate human psycholog-ical and physiological wellbeing through recovery from directed attention and stress. It also revealed aspects of the ambient mountain landscape environ-ment conditions that combine to influence human physiological responses. The evidences are in threefold: experiential psychological evidence, experiential physiological evidence and ambient mountain landscape environment and physiological responses.

Experiential Psychological Evidence

The experiential psychological evidence involved the exploration of the link between perceived stress of individuals in the urban environment and their perceived restorativeness in the mountain landscape environment. The four components of a restorative environment namely, being away, extent, fascination and compatibility were linked to perceived stress of individuals. This established the extent of psychological recovery from directed attention and stress in the mountain landscape environment.

Being away and compatibility influenced perceived stress significantly, the extent and fascination components did not. Being away was influenced by the geographical and psychological disengagement from the everyday urban stressors by individuals. The significant influence of compatibility on the perceived stress of individuals showed that the mountain landscape environment allowed a compatible link between the perceived motive of individuals for wellbeing and availability of activities to support the wellbeing. Situating it within the context of mountain landscape environments, individual's recovery from perceived stress and restoration of directed attention was prompted by the being away and compatibility components. In addition, the multiplicity of the mountain landscape features afforded the opportunity for engagement in various activities which gave rise to compatibility feelings leading to recovery from stress. This affirms the phenomenon of being away and compatibility as an explanation for increased restorativeness and stress mitigation leading to wellbeing with regards to mountain landscape environments.

Fascination and extent did not influence perceived stress significantly. Therefore, the feeling of fascination in the mountain landscape environment does not indicate restoration from stress. However, three criteria were found in addition to being away and compatibility as components of a restorative environment with emphasis on mountains. The additional criteria are: interest, pleasantness and tranquillity. These criteria were influenced by the following attributes of the mountain landscape environment: (1) the multi-stimulus nature of the Obudu mountain landscape environment generated the kind of interest required for an individual to effectively switch the thought process from the stressful urban environment to the restorative mountain landscape environment; (2) the breath-taking view of the mountain environment as experienced by individuals from the cable car ride afforded the feeling of pleasantness; and (3) the calm and quietness of the mountain landscape environment comparared to the urban environment impacted its tranquil character. Thus, the combination of this attributes namely, being away, compatibility, interest, pleasantness and tranquil stimulates human psycho-logical wellbeing by influencing recovery from directed attention and stress.

Experiential Physiological Evidence

This study was anchored on the assumption that contact with environments possessing high restorative qualities can enhance better health benefits than contact with less restorative quality. Hence, a strategy was developed to fill the gap created by the use of psychometric self-report measures driven by consciousness, observation and mood states to determine the magnitude of psychological human response to environmental stimuli. Therefore, physio-logical outcomes of blood pressure, pulse rate and respiratory rate measure-ments yielded results that reduced the chances of subjective bias in the per-ception and reporting of responses.

Systolic blood pressure increased while diastolic blood pressure and pulse rate decreased both in individuals and across age groups in the mountain landscape environment. Individuals' inability to adapt to sudden variations in environmental configuration influenced the increase in their systolic blood pressure. Whereas, diastolic blood pressure and pulse rate decreased in the mountain landscape environment due to an attempt by the human body system to maintain balance otherwise known as homeostasis. Homeostasis was maintained through the activation of the response system by way of ad-justment and adaptation to the mountain landscape features which fostered calmness and excitement. The features included vantage point views, cascad-ing waterfalls, river, forest groves and vegetation which enhanced individual's ability to attain a relaxed state in the absence of stress stimulating features.

On the other hand, respiratory rate did not indicate any tangible differences both in individuals and across the age groups. Therefore, an individual's res-piratory rate remains stable and maintained in both urban and mountain landscape environments hence it cannot determine stressful and non-stressful events. However, comparing gender outcomes, female respiratory rate increased in the mountain landscape environment slightly while male respiratory rate decreased. Therefore, females are more vulnerable to changes in environmental configuration and less sensitive to the exciting and stress relieving features of the mountain landscape environment.

In sum, experiential contact with the mountain landscape environment in-fluenced individual's ability to attain a relaxed state through the reduction of their diastolic blood pressure and pulse rate. Also, clear physiological effects leading to recovery from stress are obtainable through short time contact, minimum of three days, within the mountain landscape environment.

Ambient Mountain Landscape Environment and Physiological Responses

Temperature and humidity are aspects of the mountain landscape environment conditions that combine to influence human physiological wellbeing. A comparison of these conditions between the urban and mountain landscape environment revealed the significance of wellbeing. While temperature decreased in the mountain landscape environment compared to the urban environment, humidity decreased. This was found to have influenced the increase in systolic blood pressure but a decrease in both diastolic blood pressure and pulse rate. Therefore, the being away component of the mountain landscape environment includes a combined psychological and physiological feeling. The feeling is aided by both the seen features (e.g. trees, vegetation, water features and undulating mountains) and unseen factors (e.g. temperature and relative humidity) of the mountain landscape environment.

Temperature and humidity are inversely but significantly associated with systolic blood pressure, diastolic blood pressure and pulse rate. Temperature and humidity was, however, inversely but not significantly associated with respiratory rate. The inverse association was due to the periodic fluctuations in the environmental conditions. Hence, when there is an increase in temperature and humidity, systolic blood pressure, diastolic blood pressure and pulse rate are expected to reduce depending on the time of the day. This did not happen in this study because the physiological variables (systolic blood pressure, diastolic blood pressure, pulse rate and respiratory rate) were measured once on each experimental day. Therefore, depending on the time of the day, an increase in temperature and humidity would reduce the blood pressure and pulse rate.

Conclusion

The study is underpinned by the assumption that cumulative effects of contact with environments having high restorative qualities can enhance better health benefits compared to environments with less restorative quality. The multi-dimensional approach to the link between nature experience and health outcome in a mountain landscape environment yielded finding that clarifies these assumptions. A quantitative approach was employed in exploring this assumption. The research questions were formulated based on the assumption that contact with the mountain landscape environment will stimulate restorative benefits than with the urban environment. Hence, the questions were accessed from three perspectives. The first perspective dealt with subjective psychological aspects of preference and perception of the mountain landscape features. The second perspective involved experiential psychological and physiological aspects of contact with the mountain landscape environment. And lastly, the third perspective involved the relationship between ambient environment conditions and human physiological wellbeing. To adequately address the foregoing, survey and experimental research designs were deployed in extracting data from urban dwellers that constituted the study sample. Therefore, measurement strategies involving subjective questionnaires and objective equipment were used. Descriptive and inferential statistics were carried out across the measurement strategies with the aid of statistical package for the social sciences (SPSS) software.

From the multidimensional methodology employed, an in-depth assessment of the phenomenon of restoration was achieved through the triangulation of data and results obtained from the analysis. Also, the scope of environments studied in terms of landscape types and their restorative benefits have been expanded through the situatedness of this study in the mountain landscape environment and exploration of the indicators of human psychophysiological conditions. The study concludes that contact with mountain landscape environment promotes spontaneous recovery from stress and restoration of directed attention.

References

Abdulla, K. and Taka, M. (1988). Climatic effects on blood pressure in normotensive and hypertensive subjects. *Postgraduate Medical Journal.* 64(747), 23-26.

Beil, K. and Hanes, D. (2013). The influence of urban natural and built environments on physiological and psychological measures of stress—A pilot study. *International Journal of Environmental research and Public health.* 10(4), 1250-1267.

Bell, P. A., Green, T., Fisher, J. D. and Baum, A. (2001). Environmental Psychology. (4th ed) Fort Worth.

Bergdahl, J. and Bergdahl, M. (2002). Perceived stress in adults: prevalence and association of depression, anxiety and medication in a Swedish population. *Stress and Health.* 18(5), 235-241.

Berman, M. G., Jonides, J. and Kaplan, S. (2008). The cognitive benefits of interacting with nature. *Psychological Science.* 19(12), 1207-1212.

Berto, R. (2007). Assessing the restorative value of the environment: A study on the elderly in comparison with young adults and adolescents. *International Journal of Psychology.* 42(5), 331-341.

Berto, R. (2014). The role of nature in coping with psycho-physiological stress: a literature review on restorativeness. *Behavioural Sciences.* 4(4), 394-409.

Beza, B. B. (2010). The aesthetic value of a mountain landscape: A study of the Mt. Everest Trek. *Landscape and Urban Planning.* 97(4), 306-317.

Biaggioni, I. (2008). Circadian clocks, autonomic rhythms, and blood pressure dipping. *Hypertension.* 52(5), 797-798.

Bratman, G. N., Hamilton, J. P. and Daily, G. C. (2012). The impacts of nature experience on human cognitive function and mental health. Annals of the New York Academy of Sciences. 1249(1), 118-136.

Bratman, G. N., Daily, G. C., Levy, B. J. and Gross, J. J. (2015). The benefits of nature experience: Improved affect and cognition. *Landscape and Urban Planning.* 138, 41-50.

Brown, D. K., Barton, J. L. and Gladwell, V. F. (2013). Viewing nature scenes positively affects recovery of autonomic function following acute-mental stress. *Environmental Science & Technology.* 47(11), 5562-5569.

Bulut, Z., Karahan, F. and Sezen, I. (2010). Determining visual beauties of natural waterscapes: A case study for Tortum Valley (Erzurum/Turkey). *Scientific Research and Essay.* 5(2), 170-182.

Chang, C.-Y., Hammitt, W. E., Chen, P.-K., Machnik, L. and Su, W.-C. (2008). Psychophysiological responses and restorative values of natural environments in Taiwan. *Landscape and Urban Planning.* 85(2), 79-84.

Chen, Q., Wang, J., Tian, J., Tang, X., Yu, C., Marshall, R. J., Chen, D., Cao, W., Zhan, S. and Lv, J. (2013). Association between ambient temperature and blood pressure and blood pressure regulators: 1831 Hypertensive patients followed up for three years. PloS one. 8(12), e84522.

Cohen, S., Kamarck, T. and Mermelstein, R. (1983). A global measure of perceived stress. J*ournal of Health and Social Behaviour.* 385-396.

Creswell, J. W. (2012). *Educational research: Planning, Conducting, and Evaluating Quantitative.* (4th ed.) Prentice Hall: US.

Creswell, J. W. (2013). *Research design: Qualitative, Quantitative, and Mixed methods approaches.* Sage publications Inc.: US.

Creswell, J. W. and Clark, V. L. P. (2017). *Designing and conducting Mixed methods research.* Sage Publications, Inc.: United State of America.

Cretikos, M. A., Bellomo, R., Hillman, K., Chen, J., Finfer, S. and Flabouris, A. (2008). Respiratory rate: the neglected vital sign. *Medical Journal of Australia.* 188(11), 657.

Daniel, W. W. and Cross, C. L. (2010). *Biostatistics: basic concepts and Methodology for the health sciences.* John Wiley & Sons New York.

De Greeff, A., Lorde, I., Wilton, A., Seed, P., Coleman, A. and Shennan, A. (2010). Calibration accuracy of hospital-based non-invasive blood pressure measuring devices. *Journal of Human Hypertension.* 24(1), 58-63.

Deming, M. E. and Swaffield, S. (2011). *Landscape architectural research: Inquiry, strategy, design.* New Jersey: John Wiley & Sons.

Dimitrov, D. M. and Rumrill, P. D. (2003). Pretest-posttest designs and measurement of change. Work- 2003, Medical Publishers Inc. iospress.com 20(2), 159-165.

Galindo, M. P. and Hidalgo, M. C. (2005). Aesthetic preferences and the attribution of meaning: Environmental categorization processes in the evaluation of urban scenes. International *Journal of Psychology.* 40(1), 19-27.

Groat, L. and Wang, D. (2002). *Architectural Research Methods.* New York: John Wiley & Sons.

Hall, R. (2012). Mixed methods: In search of a paradigm. Vortrag. Download (am 10.01. 2013) unter: http://www. auamii. com/proceedings_Phuket_2012/Hall. pdf.

Halonen, J. I., Zanobetti, A., Sparrow, D., Vokonas, P. S. and Schwartz, J. (2011). Relationship between outdoor temperature and blood pressure. *Occupational and Environmental Medicine*. 68(4), 296-301.

Hartig, T., Evans, G. W., Jamner, L. D., Davis, D. S. and Gärling, T. (2003). Tracking restoration in natural and urban field settings. *Journal of Environmental Psychology*. 23(2), 109-123.

Hartig, T., Korpela, K., Evans, G. W. and Gärling, T. (1996). Validation of a Measure of perceived Environmental Restorativeness. University of Göteborg, Department of Psychology.

Hartig, T., Korpela, K., Evans, G. W. and Gärling, T. (1997). A Measure of Restorative quality in Environments. *Scandinavian Housing and Planning Research*. 14(4), 175-

Hartig, T., Maris, E. and Staats, H. (1998). On relations between environmental preference and well-being. Proceedings of the 1998 15th IAPS conference, 14-17.

Hartig, T., Mitchell, R., De Vries, S. and Frumkin, H. (2014). Nature and health. Annual Review of Public Health. 35, 207-228.

Hartig, T., van den Berg, A. E., Hagerhall, C. M., Tomalak, M., Bauer, N., Hansmann, R., Ojala, A., Syngollitou, E., Carrus, G. and van Herzele, A. (2011). *Health benefits of nature experience: Psychological, Social and Cultural Processes*. In Nilsson, K., Sangster, M., Gallis, C., Hartig, T., De Vries, S., Seeland, K. & Schpperrijn, J. (Eds.) Forests, Trees and Human health (pp. 127-168) Springer.

Heale, R. and Twycross, A. (2015). Validity and Reliability in Quantitative studies. *Evidence Based Nursing*. ebnurs-2015-102129.

Herzog, T. R. and Kropscott, L. S. (2004). Legibility, mystery, and visual access as predictors of preference and perceived danger in forest settings without pathways. *Environment and Behaviour*. 36(5), 659-677.

Herzog, T. R. and Shier, R. L. (2000). Complexity, age, and building preference. *Environment and Behaviour*. 32(4), 557-575.

Hidalgo, M. C., Berto, R., Galindo, M. P. and Getrevi, A. (2006). Identifying attractive and unattractive urban places: categories, restorativeness and aesthetic attributes. *Medio Ambiente y Comportamiento Humano*. 7(2), 115-133.

Holbrook, A. (2009). The Green We Need: An Investigation of the Benefits of Green Life and Green Spaces for Urban-dwellers' Physical, Mental and Social Health. Nursery and Garden Industry Australia and SORTI, The University of Newcastle.

Horiuchi, M., Endo, J., Takayama, N., Murase, K., Nishiyama, N., Saito, H. and Fujiwara, A. (2014). Impact of Viewing vs. Not Viewing a Real Forest on Physiological and Psychological Responses in the Same Setting. *International Journal of Environmental research and Public health*. 11(10), 10883-10901.

Jamaludin, A. A., Hussein, H., Daud, N. K., Ariffin, M. and Rosemary, A. (2013). Living behaviour assessment at residential college building with bioclimatic design strategies. Retrieved from https://works.bepress.com/adiainurzaman/26/

Kaplan, R. (2001a). The nature of the view from home psychological benefits. *Environment and Behaviour*. 33(4), 507-542.

Kaplan, R. and Kaplan, S. (2011). Well-being, Reasonableness, and the Natural Environment. Applied Psychology: *Health and Well-Being.* 3(3), 304-321.

Kaplan, S. (1992). *The Restorative Environment: nature and Human experience.* In Diane, R. (Ed.) Role of Horticulture in Human Well-being and Social Development (pp. 134-142). Arlinton, Virginia: Timber press.

Kaplan, S. (1995). The restorative benefits of nature: Toward an integrative framework. *Journal of Environmental Psychology.* 15(3), 169-182.

Kaplan, R. and Kaplan, S. (1989). *The experience of nature: A psychological perspective* (First ed.). New York, United States: Cambridge University Press.

Kaymaz, I. C. (2012b). Landscape perception. In M. Ozyavuz (Ed.), *Landscape planning* (pp. 251-276). Rijeka, Croatia: Intech.

Kellert, S. R. (1995). *The Biophilia hypothesis.* New York: Island Press.

Kent, S. T., Howard, G., Crosson, W. L., Prineas, R. J. and McClure, L. A. (2011). The association of remotely-sensed outdoor temperature with blood pressure levels in REGARDS: a cross-sectional study of a large, national cohort of African-American and white participants. *Environmental Health.* 10(7).

Krauss, S. E. (2005). Research paradigms and meaning making: A primer. The qualitative report. 10(4), 758-770.

Kroh, D. P. and Gimblett, R. H. (1992). Comparing live experience with pictures in articulating landscape preference. *Landscape Research.* 17(2), 58-69.

Lather, P. (1992). Critical frames in educational research: Feminist and post-structural perspectives. *Theory into practice.* 31(2), 87-99.

Lee, H.-Y. and Oh, B.-H. (2010). Aging and arterial stiffness. *Circulation Journal.* 74(11), 2257-2262.

Lee, J., Park, B.-J., Tyrväinen, L., Li, Q., Kagawa, T., Miyazaki, Y. and Tsunetsugu, Y. (2012). *Nature therapy and Preventive Medicine.* INTECH Open Access Publisher.

Lee, J., Tsunetsugu, Y., Takayama, N., Park, B.-J., Li, Q., Song, C., Komatsu, M., Ikei, H., Tyrväinen, L. and Kagawa, T. (2014). Influence of forest therapy on cardiovascular relaxation in young adults. *Evidence based Complementary and Alternative Medicine,* Volume 2014, Article ID 834360, 7 pages http://dx.doi.org/10.1155/2014/834360

Lee, M.-s., Park, B.-j., Lee, J., Park, K.-t., Ku, J.-h., Lee, J.-w., Oh, K.-o. and Miyazaki, Y. (2013). Physiological relaxation induced by horticultural activity: transplanting work using flowering plants. *Journal of Physiological Anthropology.* 32(1), 15.

Lindemann-Matthies, P., Briegel, R., Schüpbach, B. and Junge, X. (2010). Aesthetic preference for a Swiss alpine landscape: The impact of different agricultural land-use with different biodiversity. *Landscape and Urban Planning.* 98(2), 99-109.

Madsen, C. and Nafstad, P. (2006). Associations between environmental exposure and blood pressure among participants in the Oslo Health Study (HUBRO). *European Journal of Epidemiology.* 21(7), 485-491.

Marazziti, D., Di Muro, A. and Castrogiovanni, P. (1992). Psychological stress and body temperature changes in humans. *Physiology & Behaviour.* 52(2), 393-395.

McFadden, J., Price, R., Eastwood, H. and Briggs, R. (1982). Raised respiratory rate in elderly patients: a valuable physical sign. *British Medical Journal* 284 (6316), 626-627.

McGregor, S. L. and Murnane, J. A. (2010). Paradigm, methodology and method: Intellectual integrity in consumer scholarship. *International Journal of Consumer Studies.* 34(4), 419-427.

Miller, D. (2001). A method for estimating changes in the visibility of land cover. *Landscape and Urban Planning.* 54(1), 93-106.

Mitchell, M. and Jolley, J. (2012). *Research Design Explained.* Cengage Learning.

O'Brien, E., Asmar, R., Beilin, L., Imai, Y., Mallion, J.-M., Mancia, G., Mengden, T., Myers, M., Padfield, P. and Palatini, P. (2003). European Society of Hypertension recommendations for conventional, ambulatory and home blood pressure measurement. *Journal of Hypertension.* 21(5), 821-848.

Ochiai, H., Ikei, H., Song, C., Kobayashi, M., Takamatsu, A., Miura, T., Kagawa, T., Li, Q., Kumeda, S. and Imai, M. (2015). Physiological and Psychological Effects of Forest Therapy on Middle-Aged Males with High-Normal Blood Pressure. *International Journal of Environmental research and Public health.* 12(3), 2532-2542.

Okada, M. and Kakehashi, M. (2014). Effects of outdoor temperature on changes in physiological variables before and after lunch in healthy women. *International Journal of Biometeorology.* 58(9), 1973-1981.

Onwuegbuzie, A. J. and Collins, K. M. (2007). A typology of mixed methods sampling designs in social science research. *The Qualitative Report.* 12(2), 281-316.

Park, B.-J., Tsunetsugu, Y., Ishii, H., Furuhashi, S., Hirano, H., Kagawa, T. and Miyazaki, Y. (2008). Physiological effects of Shinrin-yoku (taking in the atmosphere of the forest) in a mixed forest in Shinano Town, Japan. *Scandinavian Journal of Forest Research.* 23(3), 278-283.

Pazhouhanfar, M. and Kamal, M. (2014). Effect of predictors of visual preference as characteristics of urban natural landscapes in increasing perceived restorative potential. *Urban Forestry & Urban Greening.* 13(1), 145-151.

Pickering, T. G., Hall, J. E., Appel, L. J., Falkner, B. E., Graves, J., Hill, M. N., Jones, D. W., Kurtz, T., Sheps, S. G. and Roccella, E. J. (2005). Recommendations for blood pressure measurement in humans and experimental animals part 1: blood pressure measurement in humans: a statement for professionals from the Subcommittee of Professional and Public Education of the American Heart Association Council on High Blood Pressure Research. *Hypertension.* 45(1), 142-161.

Plarre, K., Raij, A., Hossain, S. M., Ali, A. A., Nakajima, M., al'Absi, M., Ertin, E., Kamarck, T., Kumar, S. and Scott, M. (2011). Continuous inference of psychological stress from sensory measurements collected in the natural environment. Proceedings of the 2011 Information Processing in Sensor Networks (IPSN), 2011 10th International Conference on: IEEE, 97-108.

Probst, T. M. (2013). Conducting Effective Stress Intervention Research: Strategies for Achieving an Elusive Goal. *Stress and Health.* 29(1), 1-4.

Ramsay, C. R., Matowe, L., Grilli, R., Grimshaw, J. M. and Thomas, R. E. (2003). Interrupted time series designs in health technology assessment: lessons from two systematic reviews of behaviour change strategies. *International Journal of Technology assessment in Health care.* 19(04), 613-623.

Russell, R., Guerry, A. D., Balvanera, P., Gould, R. K., Basurto, X., Chan, K. M., Klain, S., Levine, J. and Tam, J. (2013). Humans and nature: how knowing and experiencing nature affect well-being. *Annual Review of Environment and Resources.* 38, 473-502.

Schirpke, U., Hölzler, S., Leitinger, G., Bacher, M., Tappeiner, U. and Tasser, E. (2013a). Can We Model the Scenic Beauty of an Alpine Landscape? *Sustainability.* 5(3), 1080-1094.

Schirpke, U., Tasser, E. and Tappeiner, U. (2013b). Predicting scenic beauty of mountain regions. *Landscape and Urban Planning.* 111, 1-12.

Scopelliti, M. and Giuliani, M. V. (2004). Choosing restorative environments across the lifespan: A matter of place experience. *Journal of Environmental Psychology.* 24(4), 423-437.

Scott, M. and Canter, D. V. (1997). Picture or place? A multiple sorting study of landscape. *Journal of Environmental Psychology.* 17(4), 263-281.

Sharma, N. and Gedeon, T. (2012). Objective measures, sensors and computational techniques for stress recognition and classification: *A survey Computer Methods and Programs in Biomedicine.* 108(3), 1287-1301.

Sitiza, J. (2009). How valid and reliable are patient satisfaction data. An analysis of. 195, 319-328.

Snyder, J. and Allen, N. W. (1975). Photography, vision, and representation. *Critical Inquiry.* 2(1), 143-169.

Song, C., Ikei, H., Kobayashi, M., Miura, T., Taue, M., Kagawa, T., Li, Q., Kumeda, S., Imai, M. and Miyazaki, Y. (2015a). Effect of Forest Walking on Autonomic Nervous System Activity in Middle-Aged Hypertensive Individuals: A Pilot Study. *International Journal of Environmental research and Public health.* 12(3), 2687-2699.

Stoll-Kleemann,, S. (2015) *Local Perceptions and Preferences for Landscape and Land Use in the Fischland-Darß-Zingst Region, German Baltic Sea,* Universitat Greifswald. Institut für Geographie und Geologie.

Tsunetsugu, Y., Lee, J., Park, B.-J., Tyrväinen, L., Kagawa, T. and Miyazaki, Y. (2013). Physiological and psychological effects of viewing urban forest landscapes assessed by multiple measurements. *Landscape and Urban Planning.* 113, 90-93.

Tveit, M. S. (2009). Indicators of visual scale as predictors of landscape preference; a comparison between groups. *Journal of Environmental Management.* 90(9), 2882-2888.

Tyrväinen, L., Ojala, A., Korpela, K., Lanki, T., Tsunetsugu, Y. and Kagawa, T. (2014). The influence of urban green environments on stress relief measures: A field experiment. *Journal of Environmental Psychology.* 38, 1-9.

Uduma-Olugu, N. (2013). Perception of Suitability of Landscape Features of the Lagos Lagoon for Tourism by its Users and Users of Lagos Coastal Tourism Venues. *International Journal of Sciences.* 2(2013-07), 37-46.

Ulrich, R. S. (1979). Visual landscapes and psychological well-being. *Landscape Research.* 4(1), 17-23.

Ulrich, R. S. (1986). Human responses to vegetation and landscapes. *Landscape and Urban Planning*. 13, 29-44.

van den Berg, A. E., Jorgensen, A. and Wilson, E. R. (2014). Evaluating restoration in urban green spaces: Does setting type make a difference? *Landscape and Urban Planning*. 127, 173-181.

van den Berg, A. E., Koole, S. L. and van der Wulp, N. Y. (2003). Environmental preference and restoration:(How) are they related? *Journal of Environmental Psychology*. 23(2), 135-146.

Waghmare, M. and Chatur, P. (2012). Temperature and Humidity Analysis using Data Logger of Data Acquisition System: An Approach. *International Journal of Emerging Technology and Advanced Engineering*. 2(1), 102-106.

Waterhouse, J., Reilly, T. and Edwards, B. (2004). The stress of travel. *Journal of Sports Sciences*. 22(10), 946-966.

Weathington, B. L., Cunningham, C. J. and Pittenger, D. J. (2010). *Research Methods for the Behavioural and Social sciences*. New Jersey, United States: John Wiley & Sons.

Werner, J. (2008). Process-and controller-adaptations determine the physiological effects of cold acclimation. *European Journal of Applied Physiology*. 104(2), 137-143.

Wilkie, S. and Stavridou, A. (2013). Influence of Environmental preference and Environment type congruence on judgments of restoration potential. *Urban Forestry & Urban Greening*. 12(2), 163-170.

Wilson, E. O. (1984). *Biophilia*. Cambridge, United States: Harvard University Press.

Zohrabi, M. (2013). Mixed method research: Instruments, validity, reliability and reporting findings. *Theory and Practice in Language Studies*. 3(2), 254-262.

Appendix A

UTM
UNIVERSITI TEKNOLOGI MALAYSIA

This questionnaire is strictly for research purposes and all responses are confidential and the data collected is to support my PhD research project titled "**psychophysiological benefits of mountain landscape environment as stimulus for directed attention restoration and stress mitigation**". This study is concerned with identifying the feature(s) of the mountain environment that is potentially critical to human perception and psycho-physiological response.

Please understand that although you will not be individually identified with your questionnaire or responses and the data will be limited to this research as authorized by the Universiti Teknologi Malaysia, results may ultimately be presented in formats other than the dissertation, such as journal articles or conference presentation. If you have any concerns or queries about this questionnaire please feel to contact Henry Ojobo (07019055710) or email: global_bpc@yahoo.com.

Thank you very much for your cooperation.

Henry Ojobo (Researcher)

UniversitiTeknologi Malaysia

SECTION A- A few questions about yourself. Please tick √ the appropriate box or write where applicable.

1.   Gender: Male ○   Female ○

2.   Age (years): 21 — 30 ○   31 — 40 ○   41 — 50 ○   51 — 60 ○   61 and above ○

3.   Marital status: Married ○   Single ○

4.   Nationality: Nigerian ○   Other ○

5.   Occupation:

   ○ Government sector

   ○ Lecturer

   ○ Student

   ○ Self employed

   ○ Unemployed

   ○ Others ....

SECTION B: PREFERENCE

7.   The pictures projected below show different kinds of features present in a mountain landscape environment. You are expected to rate them in order of **PREFERENCE** by writing any of the numbers in the scale between 1 to 5 in the white box   at the corner of each picture.

1	2	3	4	5
Not preferred	Slightly preferred	Neutral	Preferred	Highly preferred

RIVER FEATURE

FOREST FEATURE

BUILT STRUCTURES FEATURE

WATERFALL FEATURE

MOUNTAIN VANTAGE POINT FEATURE

ARTIFICIAL WATER PARK FEATURE

SECTION C: PERCEPTION

8. Have you been in an environment with any of these features before? Please tick √ one or more of the options that conform to you:|

- ◯ River
- ◯ Forest
- ◯ Built structures
- ◯ Waterfall
- ◯ Mountain vantage point
- ◯ Artificial water park
- ◯ None

9. What do you perceive to be the benefit of your contact with the landscape features shown in section B? Circle a number that best reflects your perception:

	Strongly Disagree	Disagree	Neutral	Agree	Strongly Agree
Calmness	1	2	3	4	5
Relief	1	2	3	4	5
Anxiousness	1	2	3	4	5
Excitement	1	2	3	4	5

End of questions

Thank you!

Chapter 3

Spatial statistical techniques for measuring the control and management of epidemics in urban environmental neighbourhood

Emmanuel Umaru Tanko

Department of Urban and Regional Planning, Federal University of Technology Minna, Nigeria

eumaru@futminna.edu.ng

Abstract: Urban areas have been ravaged with diverse kinds of epidemics of disease in the past. Some of these diseases are associated with the urban environmental factors which aid in its spread. Several efforts have been made by governments, non-governmental organizations and individuals to curb some of the disease epidemics but not much has been achieved. This research explored the spatial statistical techniques that can be adopted in the management and prevention of epidemics of disease in urban areas. Getis and Ords hot spatial analysis was used to identify locations that have a high occurrence of the disease. Since most of the disease epidemics are associated with the urban environmental factors, geographically weighted regression model (GWR) which has the capability to investigate the relationship of the disease with the factors that aid its spread was used. Results show that the locations that have statistically significant high and low occurrence of the disease spread stood out. Geographically weighted regression model further reveals the specific factors that aid in the spread of the disease at various locations with the statistical level of significance. The study recommends that the spatial statistical methods are significantly appropriate in the management and preventions measures for disease epidemics in urban areas.

Key Words: Epidemics, Spatial, Meningococcal, Meningitis, Statistical techniques

Introduction

Meningococcal meningitis bacteria resides in human beings at different levels of dosage. It resides mostly in people that are living in the *Meningococcal meningitis* endemic regions of the world due to the fact that the bacteria reproduces and thrives very well under a favourable condition (WHO, 1998).

Most people that are living in the *Meningococcal meningitis* endemic region have the bacteria living in them, as carriers but they can never fall sick as a result of it, but they can transmit it to others when the condition is favourable to the bacteria (Moore *et al.*, 1988; Steinhoff 2007).

Environmental factors play a major role in influencing the spread of the disease as the disease is associated with poor housing condition, deprived settlements and household overcrowding (Baker *at al.*, 2000; Fone *et al.*, 2003; Olowokure *et al.*, 2006; Tully *et al.*, 2006). Other studies by Fone *et al.* (2003) and Davies *et al.* (1996) also confirmed that overcrowding and poor housing conditions are significant factors in influencing the spread of the disease. Other environmental factors like high temperature, rainfall and relative humidity play a role in the spread of the disease. Studies by Thomson *et al.* (2006); Yaka *et al.* (2008); Teyssou and Rouzic (2007) all proved that temperature, rainfall and relative humidity influences the spread of the disease.

Studying the spatial pattern of *Meningococcal meningitis* has become very critical because of the havoc that it has caused to humanity; the disease has affected every region of the world with severe cases in the developing countries, especially West Africa (WHO, 2003; Tobias *et al.*, 2011) and also northern Nigeria to be specific (Mohammed *et al.*, 2000; Sawa and Buhari, 2011). The pattern of the spread of *Meningococcal meningitis* is still very unclear to public health practitioners, epidemiologists and urban health planners, even though some of the factors that facilitate the spread are known (Bharti *et al.*, 2012). The combination of factors that could aid the spread pattern of the disease in a particular location may be different across geographical locations.

Due to Nigeria's location, within the Sub-Saharan Africa's "*Meningitis* Belt", seasonal epidemics expectedly occur in a cyclic pattern. High temperature, dusty winds, poor distribution of services in the towns and people living in an overcrowded condition has made people vulnerable to the respiratory disease and are among some of the reasons behind the *meningitis* belt's high burden of *Meningococcal* disease (Greenwood, 2006). A study carried out by Mohammed *et al.* (2000) reported that five major epidemics of *Meningococcal meningitis* occurred in the northern part of Nigeria within 30 years, in 1970, 1975, 1977, 1986, and 1996. According to that study, the epidemic of 1996 was the worst among all of them. It was followed by comparable epidemics in Chad in 1988, and that of Niger Republic in 1991 and 1994 which share their borders with Nigeria. At least 1,650 people in Nigeria have died as a result of the *Meningitis* epidemic in the northern part of the country in 1996 (Sawa & Buhari, 2011).

In spite of the nearly annual occurrences of this disease, governments do not seem to be winning the battle posed by the epidemic. Most often, outbreaks take governments unaware despite the fact that the period in which the disease is frequent is very well known. Little or no effort is made to check the spread until there is an outbreak. During epidemics, interventions are limited to the provision of vaccines to areas under attack. Thus, actions are usually taken when it is already too late and many lives have been lost. There is always a challenge in predicting the epidemics of *Meningococcal meningitis* and it normally results in the late commencement of preventive strategies, like the vaccination, which does not produce a good outcome (Greenwood *et al.*, 1984). The conventional statistical approach used in detecting and measuring the spread of diseases has not yielded much result; instead, it gives a general overview of factors responsible for the spread of diseases. This study explores some of the spatial statistical techniques that can be adopted in the management and prevention of epidemics of disease in urban areas.

Epidemics of Meningococcal Meningitis

The *Meningococcal meningitis* attack usually begins with an intense headache, vomiting and stiff neck and progresses to a coma within few hours (Varaine *et al.*, 1997). The fatality of typical untreated cases is about 80 percent. With early diagnosis and treatment, case fatality rates have declined to less than 10 percent. According to Greenwood *et al.* (1984), developing countries have accounted for a high number of the occurrences of *Meningococcal* disease with a proportion of those carrying the disease and the ones that have been attacked fluctuating between 1:100 when there are epidemics to 1:1,000 in areas that are endemic. It suggests that people are able to evolve immunity, naturally to this disease in areas that are prone to the bacteria that causes it. There might be little level of natural immunity in regions of little endemicity. Most of the people travelling from regions of low endemicity to regions of high endemicity especially the residents of Europe travelling to some areas in Africa, the Indian sub-continent and some other areas in Asia, parts of Middle East and the South America would therefore be susceptible to *Meningococcal* disease (LaForce *et al.*, 2007).

Harrison *et al.*, (2011) pointed out that the epidemics of *Meningococcal meningitis* is evident everywhere in the world (Figure 3.1), and it is observed in some countries like Europe, America and Asia that there is an increase in the spread of the disease and also a display of the epidemiological impression which is described with the consistent outbreaks and frequent endemic occurrence of the disease in a sporadic manner. From 1970 to 1971, the cases of the disease were witnessed in Italy, Spain, Yugoslavia, and Portugal and in between 1971 to 1972 in Belgium. It was 1974 in Argentina, 1974 to 1975 in the United Kingdom and with a rapid increase in the cases in France between 1973 and 1978. There were reported cases of *Meningococcal meningitis* from Cuba between 1982 and 1984, Chile was in 1986 and 1993 (Jafri et al., 2013).

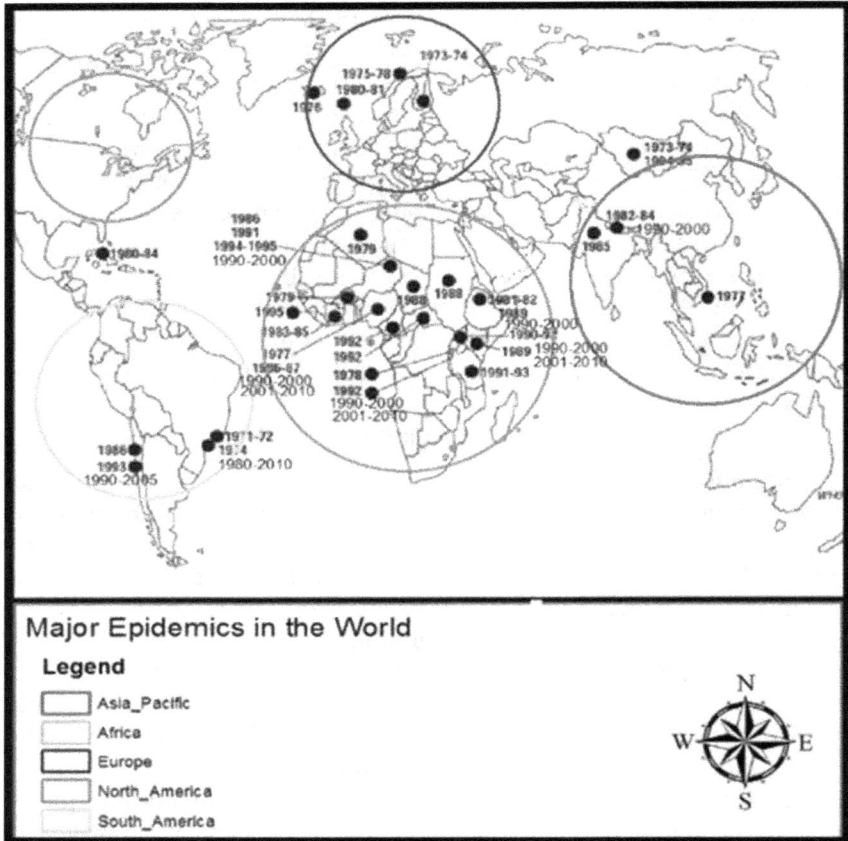

Figure 3.1 Adapted Map of the world showing locations of *Meningococcal meningitis* (Source: WHO 2003)

Spatial Epidemiology

Spatial epidemiology deals with studying the spatial spread of incidences of disease and the relationships with factors that contribute to the disease spread. Having an understanding of the spatial and temporal changes of the disease and categorizing the spatial structure is very important for the health planners to have a clear knowledge of the population's interaction with the immediate environment. The source of spatial epidemiology is John Snow and dates back to 1855 with the study he conducted on the spread of cholera in London (Osie, 2010).

Buyong (2007) defined spatial data analysis as the statistical study of phenomena that manifests them in space. This makes location, area, topology, spatial arrangement, distance and interaction the focus of attention. Spatial data analysis focuses mainly on the spatial aspects of the data in the area of spatial dependence and spatial heterogeneity. The techniques' main objective is to describe spatial distributions, discover patterns of spatial association (clustering), suggest different spatial regimes or other forms of spatial instability (non-stationary) and identify typical observations (Anselin, 1988).

In the conventional statistics, the methods developed are only applicable to the attributes components of the spatial data, but different methods are required for the treatment of the spatial components of spatial data. Waller and Gotway (2004) pointed out that in health research; spatial analysis is used to detect and quantify patterns of disease distribution that may offer insights into disease epidemiology. Spatial analysis is designed to detect clusters of health events and demonstrate significant areas of either high or low disease risk. The concept tends to look at how observations that are located near each other are influenced by each other and it is not distributed in space or time by random chance alone (Meade and Earickson, 2000). The advantage of detecting clusters is to identify spatial patterns that are unique and different than what could be expected in the absence of the phenomenon being studied and this makes clustering to be the measure of an areas abnormality relative to a null expectation (Fotheringham *et al.*, 2002).

Spatial Pattern Analysis in Epidemiological Studies

A number of studies conducted using the spatial pattern analysis show that it is helpful in determining the locations of high and low incidence of diseases. A study by Zhang *et al.* (2008) investigated the spatial pattern of malaria in a province in China because it was the most affected in the whole of China from 2005 – 2006. It was very critical to understand the pattern of spread so as to identify those locations that have high cases for future public health planning and resource allocation. Spatial cluster analysis using spatial scan statistics techniques was used. The result shows that some particular counties were at high risk for malaria.

Similarly, a study by Yeshiwondim *et al.* (2009) also investigated the spatial and temporal pattern of malaria incidence at a village in Ethiopia. Global moran's I and the anselin local spatial autocorrelation statistics were used to analyse the malaria data. The anselin local spatial autocorrelation statistics reveals clustering or hotspots within five and ten kilometres distance from the villages in the study area. It was observed that there were temporal; variations in the malaria incidence. The study could not identify those environmental factors that influence the incidence of malaria. In the same line, Srivastava *et al.* (2009) conducted a study on the identification of malaria hotspots for focused intervention in India. The purpose of the research was to identify the location of the high spot so that the authorities will focus their attention on such areas. Hot spot analysis was conducted and those areas with high cases of the disease were identified and more attention was to be given to them in order to mitigate the high cases of the disease. However, identification of factors that influence the spread of the disease was not considered by the study.

The spatial pattern analysis method was also applied to the schistosomiasis disease in China. The study was conducted by Hu *et al.* (2013), on the spatial pattern of schistosomiasis in Xingzi in the province of Jiangxi in China. Xingzi is a location where the disease of schistosomiasis had been a threat to public health. Logistic regression model and variogram techniques were used in the study. The results revealed that in those locations the disease was common and it had a spatial pattern. This finding helped in giving an insight on the characteristics of the epidemiology of the disease and would assist in the long term sustainable strategies for schistosomiasis control. Further studies were conducted on the spatial pattern of schistosomiasis in Yangtze river valley by Hu *et al.* (2014) between the years of 1991 – 2001 and 2007 – 2008. Luc anselin local spatial autocorrelation and Kuldorf spatial scan statistics were used in the study. The result showed that the magnitude and number of clusters varied from 1999 – 2001. The finding specifically showed those locations that have consistent cases which the public health planners and authorities concerned were expected to direct their attention towards. However, the limitation of the study is its inability to identify factors that were influencing the high cases of the disease.

There were also studies on spatial pattern analysis conducted for the epidemiology of *Meningococcal meningitis*. Hoebe *et al.* (2004) used space time cluster analysis to investigate the invasive *Meningococcal* disease in the Netherlands. The cluster analysis method that was used is the space-time nearest neighbour analysis. It was discovered that the clustering which was beyond chance took place between the neighbours in close range with each other. The study was able to locate those areas where higher cases of the disease were more apparent, but it could not quantify the extent of the clustering. A similar study was conducted by Greene *et al.* (2005) to investigate the Spatio-temporal pattern of viral *meningitis* in Michigan. The research showed that blacks and infants were found to be the risk group. The cases of the disease were found to be concentrated on the southern part of the study area. Spatio-temporal clusters were identified from 1998-2001. Similarly, the study could not identify those local and socio-demographic factors that influenced the spread of the disease. Philippon *et al.* (2009) in a study to investigate the spatial pattern of *Meningococcal meningitis* in Mali could also not identify the potential factors that influence the spread of the disease.

To further buttress the applicability of spatial pattern analysis in the epidemiology of *Meningococcal meningitis*, another study by Maïnassara *et al.* (2010) on spatial cluster occurrence and spatio-temporal evolution of the *Meningococcal* disease in Niger was conducted. Satscan using Poisson model was used to calculate the relative risk of occurrence of spatial clusters. Spatial clusters were detected at the south-eastern part of the country in the year 2002-2003. Clusters were found in the following years at the exact location as those detected in 2002-2003. Statistically significant Spatio-temporal patterns were discovered within the study years. This study too only identified the location of high clusters and the pattern of transmission of the disease but could not show any relationship between the factors that influence the spread of the disease and those locations.

In the same country (Niger), Paireau *et al.* (2012) conducted another study on the spatio-temporal clustering of *Meningococcal meningitis*. The study was conducted with the hope of gaining an understanding of the epidemiology of the disease in the whole country so as to improve the control strategies. Anselin local Moran's I test for spatial autocorrelation and Kuldorf's spatial scan statistics were used to identify the spatial and spatio-temporal clusters of cases. It was observed that there were spatial clusters every year (2003-2004) and the consistent cases were more on the southern districts of Niger. The study has shown the strength of spatial pattern analysis in detecting the clusters of *Meningococcal meningitis*, but it also could not show the relationship between the clusters and the factors that may be responsible.

Geographically Weighted Regression Modelling in Epidemiological Studies

A study by Lin and Wen (2011) investigated if spatial heterogeneity exists in the relationship of dengue mosquito and dengue-human relationship within a certain area. Ordinary least square (OLS) and geographically weighted regression (GWR) models were used to analyse the spatial relationship and also to identify the spatial heterogeneities through the use of some data of entomology and the cases of dengue in Kaohsiung and Fengshan in 2002. The findings in the study showed that dengue-mosquito and dengue-human relationship were significantly spatially non-stationary. This infers that in some areas, higher dengue incidence was related to higher vector/host densities, while in some areas higher incidences were associated with lower vector/host densities. The study shows clearly how GWR model can be used to spatially differentiate the relationships of dengue incidence with immature mosquito and human densities.

Gilbert and Chakraborty (2011) conducted another study in the application of GWR for environmental justice analysis. The past research on environmental justice was narrow with very simple assumptions in measuring health risk and also the traditional regression methods failed to clearly discern spatial variation in the statistical variation of the statistical relationship. The objective of the study was to assess if the potential health risk as a result of exposure to hazardous air pollutants is related to race/ethnicity with socioeconomic level. And also, to check how the significance of the statistical relationship between health risk/ethnicity or socio-economic status vary across the state. The findings in the study showed that race and ethnicity are significantly related to cancer risk in Florida. The study also discovered that conventional regression can cover critical local variation in the statistical relationship that is relevant to the environmental justice analysis.

Chen and Truong (2012) examined the extent to which the relationship between city disadvantages and the disease of obesity varies over geographic space. Multi-levels models were integrated with geographically weighted regression so as to examine the spatially varying relationship of obesity and area disadvantages. Body mass index was used as the dependent variable while the explanatory variable was the disadvantage index which is made up of minority composition, poverty level, and social disorder. Included also is the individual socio-demographic characteristics which accounted for the compositional effect. The result showed that the relationship between township disadvantages and high obesity was discovered to be area specific. Heterogeneity of place-level determinants of obesity was discovered across the geographical area.

Another study was undertaken by Chalkias *et al.* (2013) on the geographically heterogeneity of the relationship between obesity in childhood and the socio-environment. In the study, GWR model showed that areas that were defined by high population density, low education level, low family income and a narrow coverage of recreational areas represented an "obesogenic" environment. The benefit derived from using this model is its help to identify the causal factors.

Procedures and Methods

The data utilised in this study includes locations of the refuse dump and locations of hospitals. The total number of all the refuse dumps and the hospitals (primary health care and secondary healthcare) for each of the neighbourhoods were collected, aggregated and recorded in the polygon. Based on the literature reviewed, poor housing condition was found to influence the occurrence of *Meningococcal meningitis*. Consequently, housing condition information sought was categorized into four parts in which the buildings within the study area falls into any of the four.

I. Housing condition 1, structure is fit for purpose

II. Housing condition 2, structure is fit for purpose with sign of deterioration

III. Housing condition 3, structure is not fit for purpose, can be fixed

IV. Housing condition 4, structure not fit for purpose, needs to be demolished

Based on the documents reviewed on the factors that influence urbanization sourced from the Ministry of Economic Planning Kaduna, Nigeria, the following were considered for this research.

I. Population density for the neighbourhoods

II. Housing ownership for each neighbourhood

III. Percentage of occupation in each of the neighbourhoods

Data on *Meningococcal meningitis* cases were collected from the hospitals and clinics that are within Kaduna Urban Area between the months of January to December from 2007 to 2011.

The research was conducted in Kaduna Urban Area located within Kaduna, the capital of Kaduna state in Nigeria, which also falls within the "Africa Meningitis Belt". Kaduna Urban Area is made up Kaduna north and Kaduna south local governments, part of Chikun local government and part of Igabi local governments. The extent of Kaduna Urban Area (KUA) is approximately a rectangle measuring 40km by 30km lying roughly northeast/southwest with the heart of Kaduna in its centre (Lock, 2010). Figure 3.2 is the map of Kaduna Urban Area showing the four local governments and the twenty-four districts under the study area.

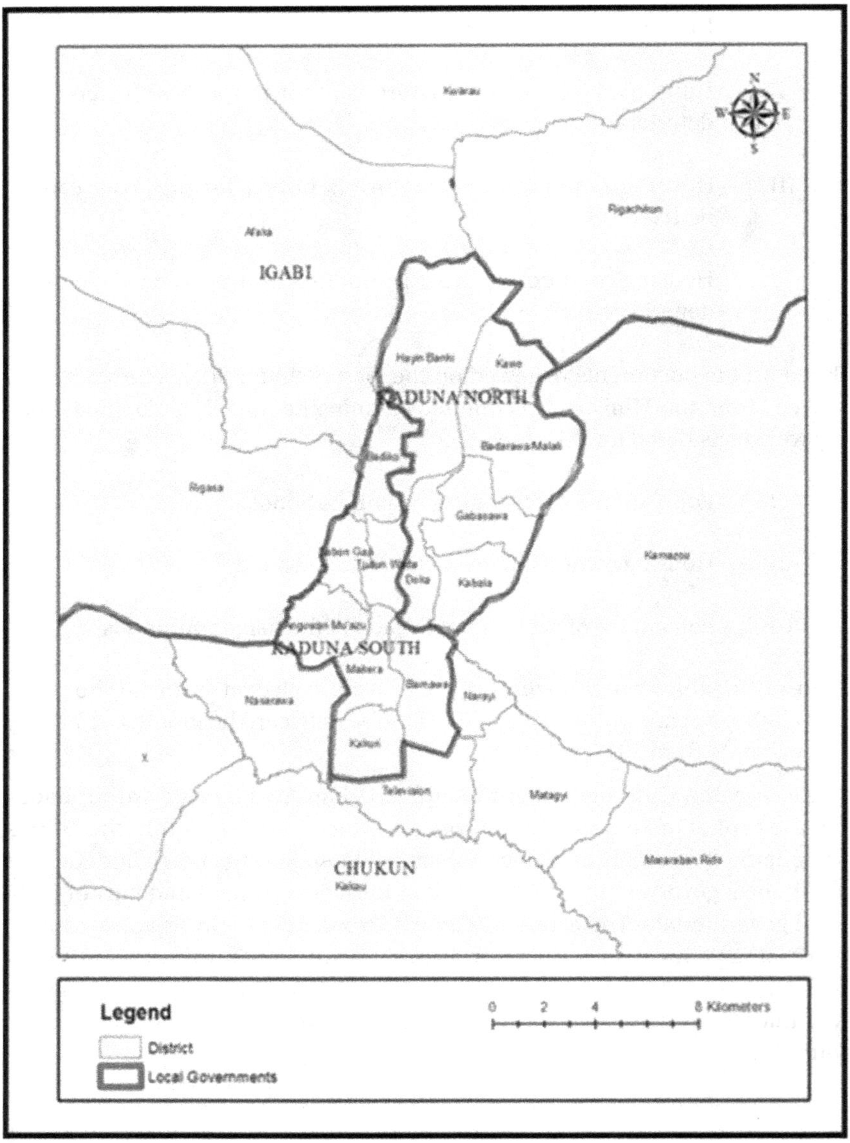

Figure 3.2 Map of Kaduna Urban Area Showing the Local Governments and 24 Districts

Spatial Pattern Analysis

Spatial pattern analysis was used in this study to determine if the incidence of *Meningococcal meningitis* in KUA conforms to a particular pattern which can either be clustered, dispersed or random and the statistical level of significance of the pattern was also identified. The spatial pattern analysis method used is the local spatial autocorrelation. Getis and Ord Local Gi* Statistics was used because it revealed the neighbourhoods that had high and low concentration of the incidence of *Meningococcal meningitis*. And also, to show the clusters' statistical significance level of the concentration either high or low. Spatio-temporal pattern analysis was conducted to determine the trend of the incidence of *Meningococcal meningitis* in KUA. Figure 3.3 shows the model of the spatial pattern analysis used for the study.

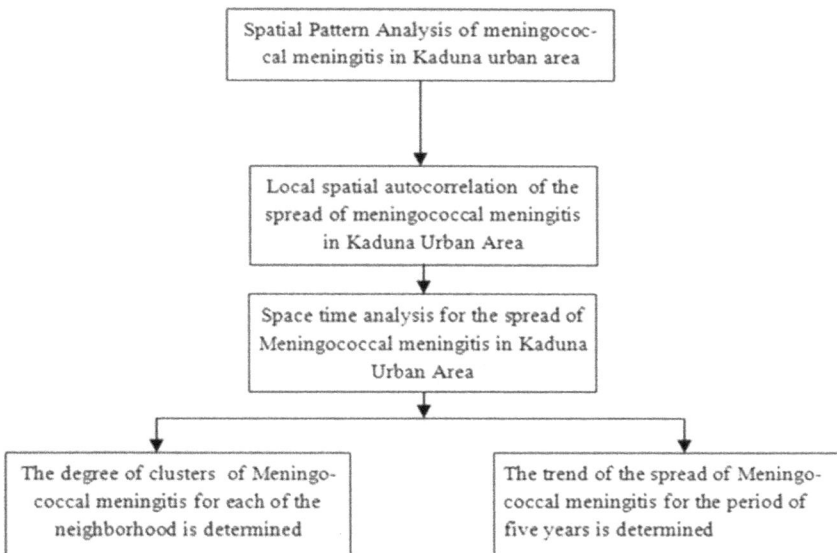

Figure 3.3 Flow chart for the Spatial Pattern Analysis Methods

Modelling the Spatial Relationships of *Meningococcal Meningitis* in Kaduna Urban Area

Geographically weighted regression (GWR) is among the various techniques of spatial regression that is being used in spatial statistics. GWR gives the local model of the variable that is being investigated or that is to be predicted by having a regression equation for each feature in the set of data. Each of the equation is put together by GWR, both the dependent and explanatory variable of the features that fall within the bandwidth of the targeted feature. Such a technique of GWR has the capacity to estimate the relationship between dependent and independent variable locally. Thus, determining the risk factors that influence the spread of *Meningococcal meningitis* peculiar to Kaduna Urban Area was easily achieved. The technique was also used to investigate the relationship of each of the factors that influence the incidence of the disease on each neighbourhood. The outcome showed the extent to which each of those factors influenced the incidence of the disease in each of the neighbourhoods. Figure 3.4 is the flow chart for the spatial relations modelling of *Meningococcal meningitis* in KUA.

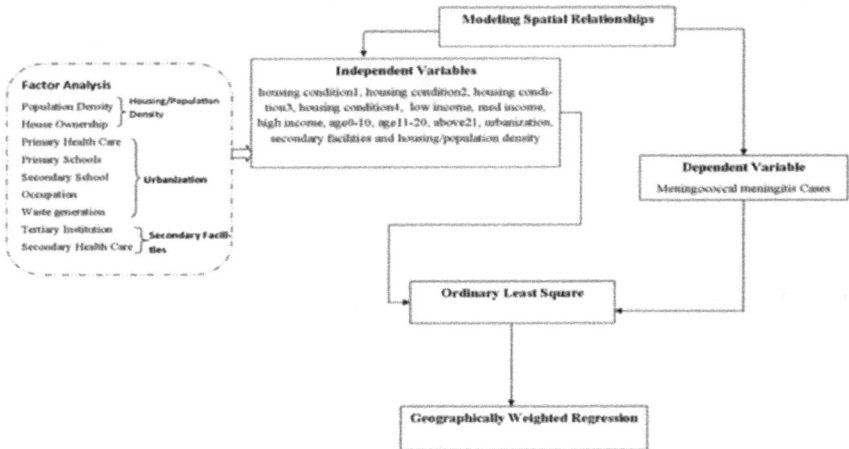

Figure 3.4 Flow chart for modelling spatial relationship for *Meningococcal meningitis* in KUA

Spatial Pattern and Temporal Analysis

Getis and Ord Gi* local spatial autocorrelation analysis was conducted in KUA with the 106 neighbourhoods. The map in Figure 3.5 (a) shows that there is a cluster of neighbourhoods with high incidences of *Meningococcal meningitis* in the neighbourhoods that are located at the south-western part of Kaduna Urban Area for year 2007. Some of the neighbourhoods with the clusters fell on the high cluster region with a standard deviation of 1.65-2.58 indicating that the clusters of high concentration of *Meningococcal meningitis* in those neighbourhoods are statistically significant. Those neighbourhoods with the z score greater than 2.58 were considered significant at 99% confidence level (p <0.01) and they are placed under the hotspot category. Neighbourhoods with z score between 1.65-1.96 and 1.96-2.58 are significant at 90% and 95% confidence level (p<0.10 and 0.05) respectively were categorized as neighbourhoods with a high risk of *Meningococcal meningitis*. The other neighbourhoods fell within the z score of -1.65 to 1.65 indicating that there was no statistically significant spatial association of neighbourhoods with the high or low *Meningococcal meningitis* incidence. Therefore, there is a pattern for the incidence of *Meningococcal Meningitis* in KUA.

Some of the neighbourhoods especially the ones that fell on the locations where there is a statistically significant pattern of the incidence of *Meningococcal meningitis* have inadequate urban facilities and services. Such neighbourhoods include Tudun-Wada, Sabon-Gari, Nasarawa, Tudun-Nupawa and Kakuri which all fell on the central and towards the south-western part of KUA. Other characteristics of such locations include high density residential neighbourhoods and poor housing conditions.

In 2008 there was a shift of the high concentration of neighbourhoods with *Meningococcal meningitis* incidences from south-western part of KUA to south-eastern part of the study area as it is shown in Figure 3.5 (b). In Figure 3.5 (c) there was a twist in the spatial pattern of the incidence of *Meningococcal meningitis* in Kaduna Urban Area for the year 2009. Unlike the other years that had only hotspot clusters, there were cold spot clusters on the spatial pattern of *Meningococcal meningitis* for year 2009. The possible reason is because 2009 was the year that the incidence of *Meningococcal meningitis* was high in the whole of West Africa and there was a reflection of that in KUA. These results match those observed in the earlier studies conducted by Jafri *et al.* (2013) and WHO (2013) which pointed out that 2009 *Meningococcal meningitis* epidemic was the highest between 2007 and 2011. Another reason could be the fact that the built environmental factors and socio-economic factors like the poor development of the urban area as a result of inadequate facilities and services, poor housing condition, high density residential neighbourhoods and low-income level were fully in existence in those locations.

The neighbourhoods that fell under the category of low clustering values are located on the south-eastern part of the study area with z score of -1.96 to -1.65 and -2.58 to -1.96 are termed as cold spot. The other neighbourhoods that fell within the z score of -1.65 to1.65 indicating that there was no statistically significant spatial association pattern of the *Meningococcal meningitis* incidence. In the year 2010, the clustering of high values of *Meningococcal meningitis* incidence was observed in the central part of KUA as shown in Figure 3.5 (d). Those neighbourhoods with a z score of >2.58 were considered significant at 99% confidence level (p<0.01) and they are under the category of hotspot. The Figure 3.5 (e) shows the incidence of *Meningococcal meningitis* in KUA for the year 2011. The neighbourhoods with a high value of clusters are located at the central part and it extends towards the south-western part of the study area.

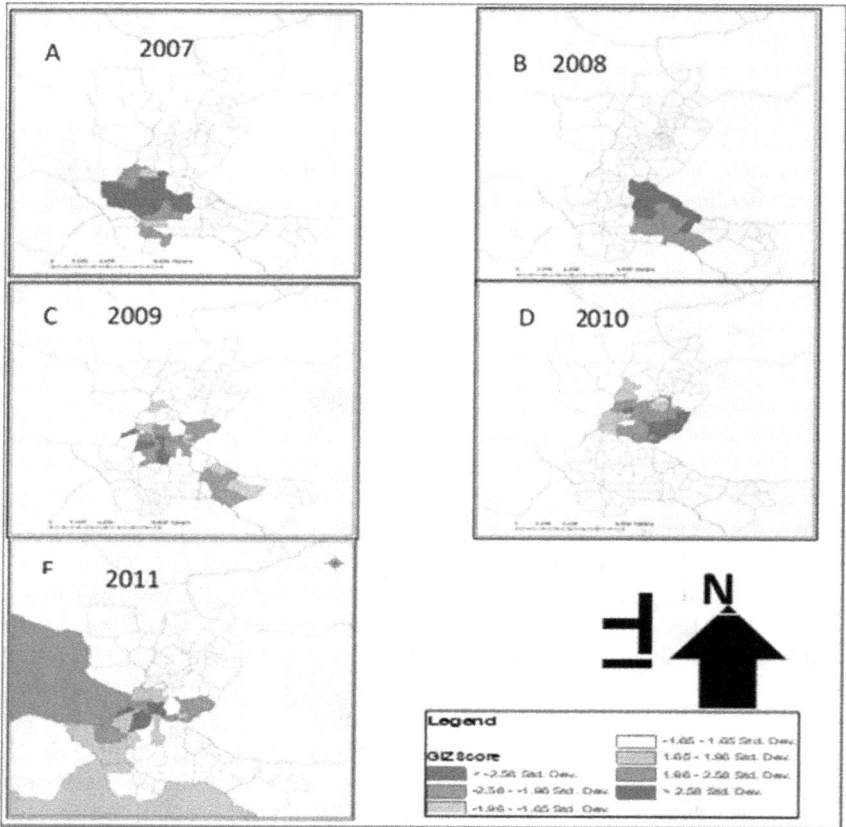

Figure 3.5 Getis and Ord Gi* Local Spatial Analysis for *Meningococcal meningitis* for KUA from year 2007 to 2011

The result of the spatial pattern analysis for the five-year period revealed that there is a pattern of the incidence of *Meningococcal meningitis* in KUA. Therefore it showed a 95% statistical confidence that the result patterns was not by chance. The findings in this study revealed the spatial pattern of *Meningococcal meningitis* incidence in KUA and the specific locations that have high and low concentrations of the disease. It was observed that in some locations there was a consistently high incidence of the disease. The consistent high concentration in the incidence of the disease was observed in neighbourhoods that are located in the central parts and also southern parts of the study area.

Comparison between OLS and GWR Models

The purpose of comparing GWR and OLS models was to identify the model with better performance. This was done by relating the model R^2 and the AICc value for both the GWR and OLS models. Recording higher R^2 means that the independent variables explain more variance in the dependent variable (Tu and Xia, 2008). While a lower AICc value indicates a closer approximation of the model reality, inferring that lower AICc means having a better model performance (Wang *et al.*, 2005). As a general rule, according to Fortheringham *et al.* (2002) and Mathews and Yang (2012), the differences of AICc between the OLS and GWR models must not be less than 3, and the model that has the lower number of not less than 3 is accepted as the better fit model. In other words, any of the models (OLS and GWR) with lower AICc value which is not less than 3 is more reliable. Supposing OLS and GWR model is ran, and the values of the AICc for the OLS is less than that of the GWR with at least (3), it is then accepted as the better fit model.

The result of the calibrated GWR indicated that there was an improvement on the OLS model. Analysing the two models together with their various AICc values revealed a drop in the value from 254.32 for the OLS model to 249.48 for the GWR model. There was a difference of about five (5) which implies that the local model fitness is greater when the spatial datasets of the incidence of *Meningococcal meningitis* is explained. The R^2 for the GWR model with an improvement of about 4 percent as shown in Table 3.1 also suggested that there was an improvement in the GWR model. About 4 percent explanation made by the GWR model was not accounted for in the OLS model which is significant in the relationship between the incidence of the disease and the variables. A study by Binbin *et al.* (2011) also had an improvement of GWR over OLS through the AICc and the R^2 because the GWR model has a better fit than the OLS model when an experiment to investigate the varying spatial relationships between house price and floor area with sample house prices in London was conducted. The study discovered that a particular locality in the study area had a strong effect on the parameter estimate.

Figure 3.6 is the map showing the local R^2 spatial smoothing of the GWR model pointing out those neighbourhoods where the model's prediction and strength of the relationship is better. The map indicates that there is a variation in the strength of the relationship in the whole of Kaduna Urban Area (KUA). The local R^2 map shows that those neighbourhoods located from some parts of the central parts towards the southern parts of KUA are having a higher R^2 which incidentally are the neighbourhoods that are more affected by *Meningococcal meningitis* disease compared with those on the northern parts of KUA. It was also observed that the spatial variation in the relationship patterns displays the intensity of relationship increasing from the northern parts to the southern parts of KUA. Hence, the variation indicates that there are local fluctuations in the relationship (non-stationary). Nonetheless, the best fit was observed in the neighbourhoods located from the central parts towards the southern parts of KUA.

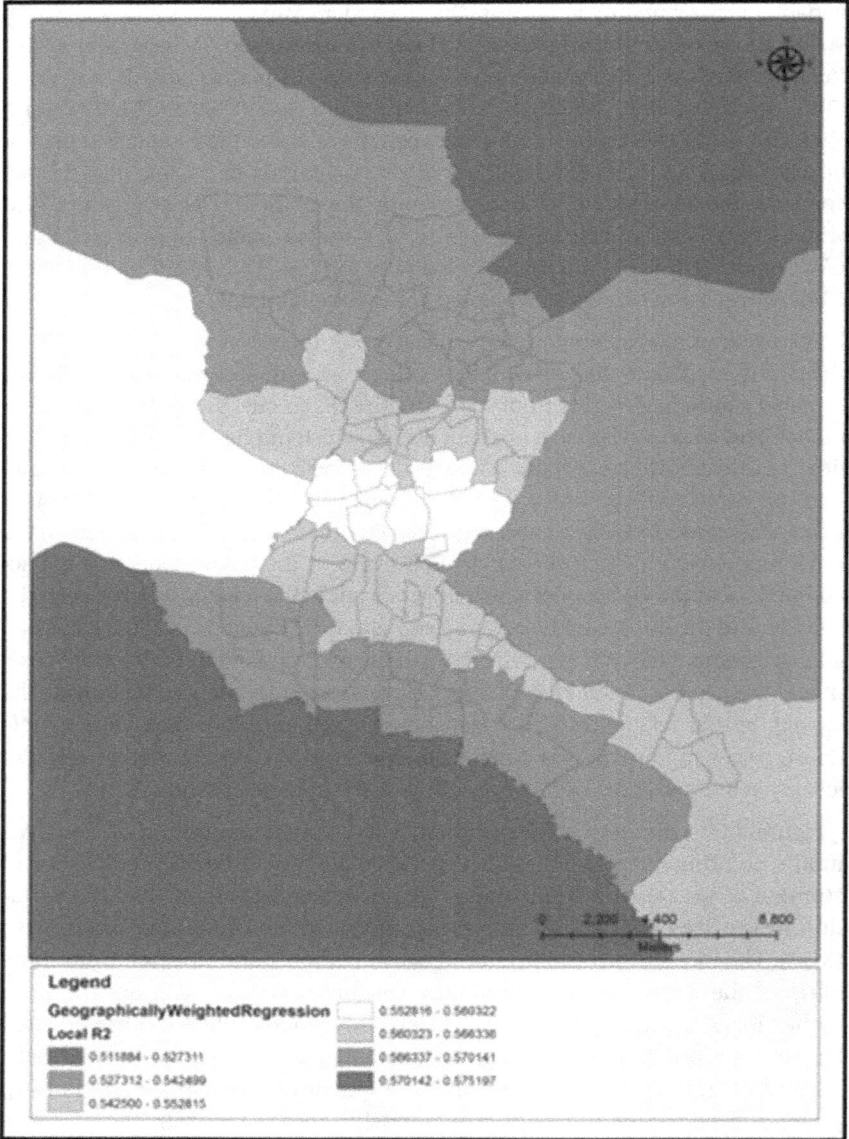

Figure 3.6 Local R² Smoothing for GWR Showing Model's Fitness Spatial Variation

Table 3.1 Summary of GWR Results

Neighbours	106
Residual Square	43.92
Effective Number	16.51
Sigma	0.69
AICc	249.48
R²	0.57
R² Adjusted	0.49

Table 3.2 Comparison between GWR and OLS

	GWR	**OLS**
AICc	249.48	254.32
R²	0.57	0.53
Adjusted R²	0.49	0.47

Parameter Estimates (coefficient) and *T*-Values

This section deals with the GWR model results. The result of the parameter estimates reveals that there are variations. These variations are not so much for all the explanatory variables and it is not all the independent variables that show a significant relationship with the incidence of *Meningococcal meningitis* in KUA. Some of the variables show variations in the relationship with some recording significant t-values. Yet some are without any significant value which gives a deeper insight into the existing local relationship of *Meningococcal meningitis* and the independent variables which OLS model could not give within KUA. The spatial varying relationship existing is known through the parameter estimates and the t-values for each of the variable. Among the eleven explanatory variables, 4 are statistically significant; these are urbanization, housing density age 0-10 and housing condition 3. These variables are the most important with respect to explaining the incidence of *Meningococcal meningitis in* KUA. This result is consistent with the fact that in Nigeria squatter settlements, overcrowded neighbourhoods and age are major determinants in the transmission of communicable diseases like *Meningococcal meningitis* (Federal Ministry of Health, 2010).

On the other hand, housing condition 4 even though was significant in OLS but was not significant in GWR is another determinant in the transmission of

Meningococcal meningitis. Good housing condition is not associated with *Meningococcal meningitis,* probably that is the reason why it fails to return a significant t-values for housing condition 1 and 2 in the OLS model. Another explanatory variable that returned an insignificant t-value is the medium income level and high-income level.

In view of the methodology of this research which indicated that the spatial variation in the relationship for dependent and independent variable and the level of significance for GWR model can be detected with the results of the parameter estimates and t-values, the result for urbanization variable in Figure 3.7 shows the result with a parameter estimates from a low value of -0.289654 to a high value of 0.179541. The neighbourhoods that have a low value for the parameter estimates are located on some parts of the central KUA and also in the north-western parts. The neighbourhoods with low value for the parameter estimates returned significant t-values. Also, the neighbourhoods with negative parameter estimates are in the areas with significant t-values which indicate the influence of urbanization. This is because the influence of urbanization on *Meningococcal meningitis* is on the inverse, implying that the less the urbanization, then the more the influence of the disease in those neighbourhoods.

The neighbourhoods that returned a significant t-values are located on the central parts of KUA and it moves towards the western parts. The parameter estimates kept decreasing as it goes towards the western parts of KUA indicating that there is variation in the spatial relationship which is due to the urbanization variable. The neighbourhoods that have inadequate facilities, poor services, absence of any physical plan and overcrowded are the ones with the negative parameter estimates which invariably influences the incidence of *Meningococcal meningitis.* The neighbourhoods within these locations include Rigasa, Tudun Wada, Anguwan Mu'azu, Nasarawa, Kakuri and Tudun Nupawa. The reason why parameter estimates are low may be connected with the fact that, it is in the low developed locations which are characterized with poor housing conditions, low income level, deprived neighbourhoods in terms of facilities and services and overcrowded environment. According to Olowukure *et al.* (2006), deprived neighbourhoods and low income are associated with the incidence of *Meningococcal meningitis.*

The result of the OLS model for housing condition 3 and 4 parameter estimate returned a significant value. The reason for this kind of result is because OLS model takes into consideration the whole study area (106 neighbourhoods) unlike the result of GWR model which is localized to each of the neighbourhoods. This implies that houses that fell under this category of housing condition 3 and 4 at the OLS model are more susceptible to the incidence of *Meningococcal meningitis* in KUA. However, the GWR model revealed that there was no significant contribution that housing condition 4 variable is making in the incidence of *Meningococcal meningitis* disease in the neighbourhoods. The parameter estimates are higher at the western parts and also in some locations on the eastern parts. These suggest that the influence of the disease even though not significant is more on the western and some parts on the eastern side.

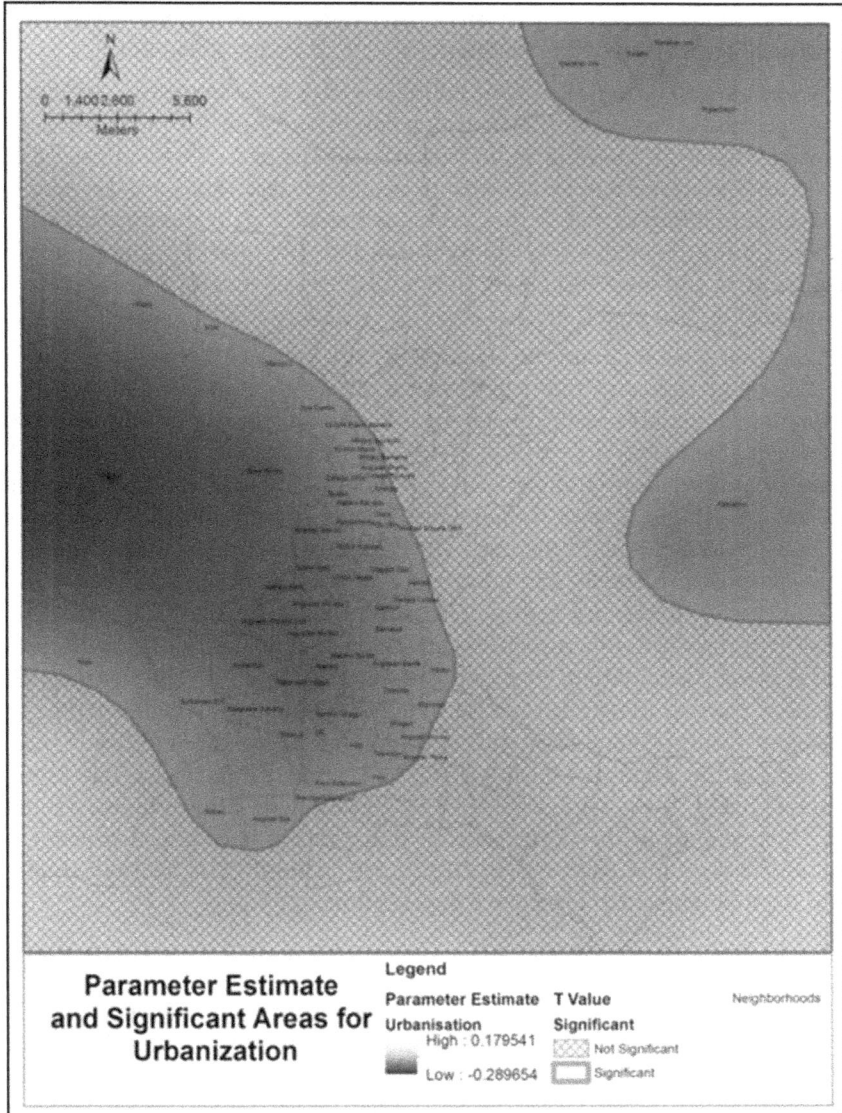

Figure 3.7 GWR Results for Urbanization

In the result of the GWR model, it was observed that housing condition 3 explanatory variable returned a significant parameter estimate of high value of 0.943612 and a low value of 0.287530 indicating that it made a significant contribution in the incidence of the disease in KUA as shown in Figure 3.7. The neighbourhoods that returned the significant parameter estimate as an indication of the existence of spatial varying relationship include Angwan Sanusi, Sabon Gari, Kabala West, Angwan Mu'azu, Kudandan, Nasarawa, Rigasa, Rigachikun, Maraban Jos, Kamazou and Bakin Ruwa.

It was observed from the result that it is where the urbanization explanatory variable is significant that housing condition 3 and 4 explanatory variables flourishes. The implication is that, inadequate facilities and services exist in "less developed area". This makes it have less value and the people that cannot afford to stay in the "developed area" usually opt for such locations. That is the reason why the housing conditions that are poor are more common in the less developed area and the incidence of *Meningococcal meningitis* is also high there.

The parameter estimates for housing density in the GWR results as shown in Figure 3.8 indicates that it returned a negative parameter estimates for explanatory variable and also, there is a significant relationship existing between *Meningococcal meningitis* and this variable. The results have indicated that there is a significant contribution that this variable makes in the incidence of *Meningococcal meningitis* in some of the neighbourhoods of KUA as it can be seen on the map- the parameter estimates value is having a high value of 0.213754 and a low value of -0.045778. The area where the parameter estimates are high indicates that there is a significant relationship. Drawing from this result, it is clear that the incidence of *Meningococcal meningitis* is influenced by housing density in KUA. The central and western parts of the study area have higher parameter estimates with significant t-values. Such neighbourhoods that fall within the significant areas include Tudun Nupawa, Makera, Doka, Angwan Barde, Barnawa, Television, Rigasa, Bakin Ruwa, Anguwan Mu'azu and Angwan Rimi. Whereas some neighbourhoods in the north-western parts do not have any significant t-value like Air force base, Malali GRA, Angwan Rimi GRA, Murtala square and Rigachukun which recorded a non-significant t-values.

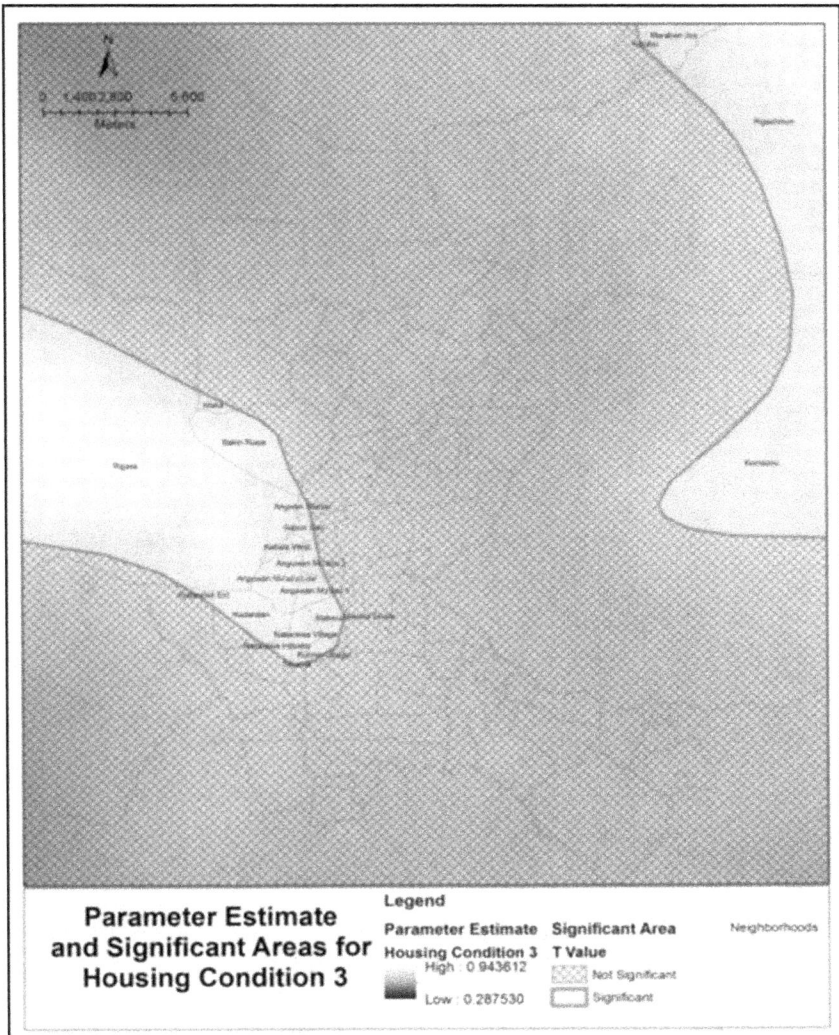

Figure 3.8 GWR Results for Housing Condition 3

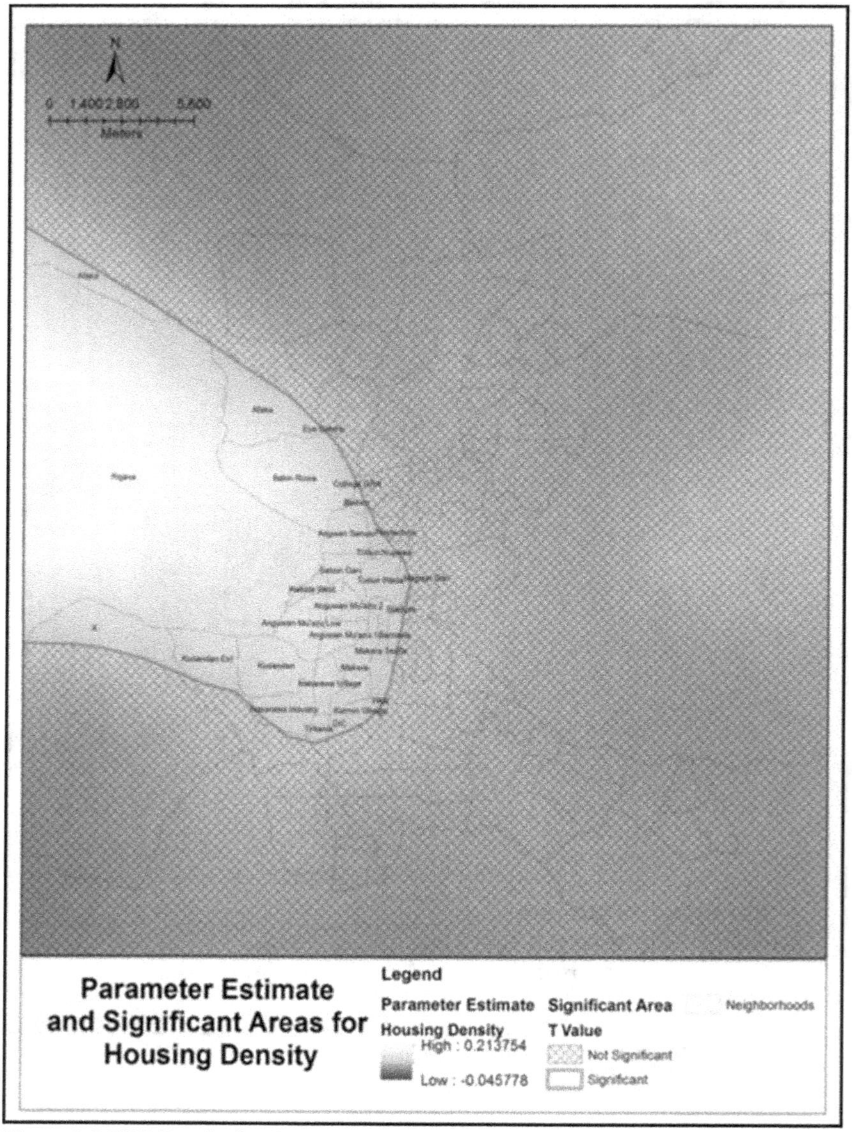

Figure 3.9 GWR Results for Housing Density

Conclusion

The findings in the spatial and temporal pattern analysis have shown the pattern and locations of concentrations of the disease. It revealed those neighbourhoods that have high and low incidences of the *Meningococcal meningitis*. This finding has pointed out the precise locations where there are high and low concentrations of the disease in KUA. Identifying those locations that the disease incidence is high will assist policy makers and health professionals to address the menace of the disease.

Ordinary Least Square (OLS) model only gives the global or general results on the relationship existing between the dependent and independent variable; the model did not specify the exact neighbourhoods where the relationship between the incidence of *Meningococcal meningitis* and all the factors are significant or less significant in KUA. It gave a general outcome showing the existence of a significant relationship between *Meningococcal meningitis* and some of the factors in the whole of KUA. The summary of the OLS means that the relationship is non-stationary because there is a local fluctuation existing in the relationships. This implies that the contribution each of the variables makes in the incidence of *Meningococcal meningitis* in KUA is not the same. It is high in some areas and low in other areas. For this reason, OLS is not the best model for explaining this kind of relationship.

The outcome of this analysis has shown that spatial data also have a non-static relationship across the geographic space when the results of OLS and GWR model fitness are compared through their parameter estimates and the t-value. Due to the potential of identifying specific relationships of dependent and independent variables across the geographic space, Geographically Weighted Regression (GWR) model is the best method. This is the peculiarity of using the local regression model (GWR) because it reveals details that are not displayed when OLS is used.

References

Anselin, L. (1988). *Spatial Econometrics: Methods and Models,Dordrecht.* (First). Arizona: Kluwer Academic Publisher.

Bharti, N., Broutin, H., Grais, R. F., Ferrari, M. J., Djibo, a, Tatem, a J., & Grenfell, B. T. (2012). Spatial dynamics of meningococcal meningitis in Niger: observed patterns in comparison with measles. *Epidemiology and Infection, 140*(8), 1356–65. http://doi.org/10.1017/S0950268811002032

Buyong, T. (2007). *Spatial Statistics for Geographical Information System.* (T. Buyong, Ed.) (First). Johor Bahru: Universiti Teknologo Malaysia.

Chalkias, C., Papadopoulos, A. G., Kalogeropoulos, K., Tambalis, K., Psarra, G., & Sidossis, L. (2013). Geographical heterogeneity of the relationship between childhood obesity and socio-environmental status: Empirical evidence from Athens, Greece. *Applied Geography, 37,* 34–43. http://doi.org/10.1016/j.apgeog.2012.10.007

Chen, D.-R., & Truong, K. (2012). Using multilevel modeling and geographically weighted regression to identify spatial variations in the relationship between place-level disadvantages and obesity in Taiwan. *Applied Geography,* *32*(2), 737–745. http://doi.org/10.1016/j.apgeog.2011.07.018

Fotheringhama, A., Stewart B. and Charlton, M. (2002). *Geographically weighted regression: The analysis of Spatially varying relationship.* John Wiley and Sons Inc.

Gilbert, A., & Chakraborty, J. (2011). Using geographically weighted regression for environmental justice analysis: Cumulative cancer risks from air toxics in Florida. *Social Science Research, 40*(1), 273–286. http://doi.org/10.1016/j.ssresearch.2010.08.006

Greene, S. K., Schmidt, M. a., Stobierski, M. G., & Wilson, M. L. (2005). Spatio-temporal pattern of viral meningitis in Michigan, 1993-2001. *Journal of Geographical Systems, 7*(1), 85–99. http://doi.org/10.1007/s10109-005-0151-x

Greenwood, B. (2006). Editorial: 100 years of epidemic meningitis in West Africa - has anything changed? *Tropical Medicine & International Health : TM & IH, 11*(6), 773–80. http://doi.org/10.1111/j.1365-3156.2006.01639.x

Greenwood BM, Blakebrough IS, Bradley AK, Wali S, W. H. (1984). Meningo-coccal disease and season in sub-Saharan Africa. *Lancet Infectious Disease, 1*, 1339–1342.

Harrison, L H Pelton, SI Wilder-Smith, A Holst, J Safadi, MAP Vazquez, JA Taha, MK LaForce, FM Gottberg, AV Borrow, R. P. S. (2011). The Global Meningococcal Initiative: Recommendations for reducing the global burden of meningococcal disease. *Vaccine, 29*, 3363–3371. http://doi.org/10.1016/j.vaccine.2011.02.058

Harrison, L. H., Trotter, C. L., & Ramsay, M. E. (2009). Global epidemiology of meningococcal disease. *Vaccine, 27 Suppl 2*, B51-63. http://doi.org/10.1016/j.vaccine.2009.04.063

Hoebe, C. J. P. a, de Melker, H., Spanjaard, L., Dankert, J., & Nagelkerke, N. (2004). Space-time cluster analysis of invasive meningococcal disease. *Emerging Infectious Diseases, 10*(9), 1621–6. http://doi.org/10.3201/eid1009.030992

Hu, Y., Xiong, C., Zhang, Z., Luo, C., Ward, M., Gao, J., ... Jiang, Q. (2014). Dynamics of spatial clustering of schistosomiasis in the Yangtze River Valley at the end of and following the World Bank Loan Project. *Parasitology International, 63*(3), 500–5. http://doi.org/10.1016/j.parint.2014.01.009

Hu, Y., Zhang, Z., Chen, Y., Wang, Z., Gao, J., Tao, B., ... Jiang, Q. (2013). Spatial pattern of schistosomiasis in Xingzi, Jiangxi Province, China: the effects of environmental factors. *Parasites & Vectors, 6*(214), 2–8. http://doi.org/10.1186/1756-3305-6-214

Jafri, R. Z., Ali, A., Messonnier, N. E., Tevi-Benissan, C., Durrheim, D., Eskola, J., ... Abramson, J. (2013). Global epidemiology of invasive meningococcal disease. *Population Health Metrics, 11*(1), 17. http://doi.org/10.1186/1478-7954-11-17

LaForce, F. M., Konde, K., Viviani, S., & Préziosi, M.-P. (2007). The Meningitis Vaccine Project. *Vaccine, 25*(1), 97–100. http://doi.org/10.1016/j.vaccine.2007.04.049

Lin, C.-H., & Wen, T.-H. (2011). Using geographically weighted regression (GWR) to explore spatial varying relationships of immature mosquitoes and human densities with the incidence of dengue. *International Journal of Environmental Research and Public Health, 8*(7), 2798–815. http://doi.org/10.3390/ijerph8072798

Maïnassara, Halima B. Nicolas Molinari2, Christophe Dematteï, P. F.-P. (2010). The relative risk of spatia cluster occurrence and spatio- temporal evolution of meningococcal disease in Niger , 2002-2008. *Geospatial Health, 5*(1), 93–101.

Meade, M. S. & Earickson, R. J. (2000). *Medical Geography* (2nd Edition). New York: The Guildford Press.

Mohammed, I., Nasidi, A., Alkali, A. S., Garbati, M. A., Ajayi-Obe, E. K., Audu, K. A., ... Abdullahi, S. (2000). A severe epidemic of meningococcal meningitis in Nigeria, 1996. *Transactions of the Royal Society of Tropical Medicine and Hygiene, 94*(3), 265–70. Retrieved from http://www.ncbi.nlm.nih.gov/pubmed/10974995

Osie, F. B. (2010). *Spatial Statistics of Epidemic Data: The case of Cholera Epidemiology in Ghana.* University of Twente.

Philippon, S., Constantin, G., Magny, D., Toure, K., Hamala, C., & Fourquet, N. (2009). Meningococcal Meningitis in Mali : a long-term study of persistence and spread. Retreived from http://doi.org/10.1016/j.ijid.2008.05.1223

Sawa, B. A., & Buhari, B. (2011). Temperature Variability and Outbreak of Meningitis and Measles in Zaria , Northern Nigeria. *Research Journal of Applied Sciences, Engineering and Technology, 3*(5), 399–402.

Srivastava, A., Nagpal, B. N., Joshi, P. L., Paliwal, J. C., & Dash, A. (2009). Identification of malaria hot spots for focused intervention in tribal state of India: a GIS based approach. *International Journal of Health Geographics, 8*(30), 1–8. http://doi.org/10.1186/1476-072X-8-30

Steinhoff, M. C. (2007). *Meningococcal Disease : Global Problem , Local Solutions.*

Teyssou, R Rouzic, E. M. (2007). Meningitis epidemics in Africa : A brief overview. *Vaccine, 25*(3–7), 7–11. http://doi.org/10.1016/j.vaccine.2007.04.032

Varaine, F., Caugant, D. a, Riou, J. Y., Kondé, M. K., Soga, G., Nshimirimana, D., ... Moren, a. (1997). Meningitis outbreaks and vaccination strategy. *Transactions of the Royal Society of Tropical Medicine and Hygiene, 91*(1), 3–7. Retrieved from http://www.ncbi.nlm.nih.gov/pubmed/9093614

Waller, L. A. and Gotway, C. (2004). *Applied Spatial Statistics for Public Health Data.* Canada: Wiley-Interscience, John Wiley and Sons.

WHO. (1998). *Control of Epidemic Meningococcal Disease. WHO Practical Guidelines. 2nd Edition.* Retrieved from http://www.path.org/vaccineresources/details.php?i=877

WHO. (2000). *Detecting Meningococcal Meningitis Epidemics in Highly-Endemic African Countries. World Health Organisation.* Retrieved from http://www.path.org/vaccineresources/details.php?i=871

Yaka, P., Sultan, B., Broutin, H., Janicot, S., Philippon, S., & Fourquet, N. (2008). Relationships between climate and year-to-year variability in meningitis outbreaks: a case study in Burkina Faso and Niger. *International Journal of Health Geographics, 7*, 34. http://doi.org/10.1186/1476-072X-7-34

Yeshiwondim, A. K., Gopal, S., Hailemariam, A. T., Dengela, D. O., & Patel, H. P. (2009). Spatial analysis of Malaria incidence at the village level in areas with unstable transmission in Ethiopia *International Journal of Health Geographics, 8*(5), 1–11. http://doi.org/10.1186/1476-072X-8-5

Zhang, W., Wang, L., Fang, L., Ma, J., Xu, Y., Jiang, J., … Cao, W. (2008). Spatial analysis of malaria in Anhui province, China. *Malaria Journal, 7,* 206. http://doi.org/10.1186/1475-2875-7-206

Chapter 4

Strategies for examining hospital spaces and family care actions towards sustainable inpatient ward setting

Alkali Ibrahim Abubakar

Faculty of Earth and Environmental Studies,
Department of Architecture, Bayero University Kano, Nigeria

abu.mahmood.00@gmail.com

Abstract: The concept of space and function is a common phenomenon in architecture and therefore forms the bedrock for spatial configuration. The relationship between space and function determines the effectiveness of an architectural product. Thus, it forms the basis for judging the success or otherwise of an architectural configuration. This applies to all building designs especially in a hospital ward setting intended to accommodate various complex and diverse functions. However, the focus in hospital design has shifted towards providing facilities that promote patient's wellbeing and restoration. Recent trends in the healthcare environment are addressed from a patient centred perspective, with concern for patients' needs and preferences. Among these major needs and preferences identified to be of significance is the social support from the patient's family. Hence the need arises on how to identify and best integrate family care activities in the hospital ward design. The variance and complexity of healthcare facilities suggests the use of critical and rigorous methods of inquiry. This provides an understanding that is evident based on how healthcare environment can be configured to promote health and wellness. This chapter thus describes the paradigms, methods, strategies and tactics employed in stimulating and exploring family care actions within a hospital ward setting.

Keywords: Hospital ward, Family, Caregiving, Inquiry strategies, sustainability

Introduction

Hospitals are a unique complex setting with various divergent components requiring special attention from the early stages of the design process. The purpose of hospitals being an environment that provides a convenient atmosphere for health care services has been the same throughout history. Despite the rapid continuous global transformation of hospitals in response to a variety of aspects of medical, social, cultural, environmental and political changes over history, the perfect hospital has not yet emerged. The development in this line introduced new paradigms and re-invent existing ones in addition to those still awaiting solution. Social support from family is one of those increasing demands. Thus, the need for scientific inquiries targeted at achieving evidence-based care and design.

Strategies used in gathering information for such inquiries in a healthcare setting depend on the goal. Owing to their variance and complexity, studies in such environments suggests the use of critical and rigorous methods of inquiry that provides an evidence-based understanding on how healthcare environment promotes or impedes health and wellness (Malagon-Maldonado, 2014). For instance, studies in the fields of Nursing, Medicine, Psychology and Architecture, revealed various strategies employed in investigating the importance of humanising and improving health care environments in order to increase users' wellbeing (Aiken *et al.*, 2012; Sadatsafavi *et al.*, 2013). Similarly, a study on the effect of healthcare environment and patients outcome (Devlin and Arneill, 2003), Physical environment stimuli that turns healthcare environment into healing environment (Dijkstra *et al,* 2006), optimising physical environment for improved outcome (Hendrich, 2003), evidence-based design for health (Lawson, 2005) and Design and the evidence (Lawson, 2013), advocate on wellbeing in health facilities.

However, previous studies have revealed that the design of healthcare facilities traditionally centres on specialties and departments rather than patients' needs (Ulrich *et al.*, 2004; Ulrich, 2007). Studies have also shown that changes made to the physical and social environment of healthcare facilities with patients as focal point results into a positive outcome. Therefore, achieving an evidence-based design in healthcare settings requires the adoption of its guiding principles (Ulrich, 1984). This has propelled an in-depth study into the impact of the physical environment of healthcare facilities on the health and wellbeing of the patients and staff (Adams, 2008; Mourshed and Zhao, 2012). Therefore, for effective healthcare facilities to be achieved, the concept of evidence-based design requires the understanding of the healthcare delivery system alongside research, design and construction processes (Debajyoti, 2011; Friedow, 2012).

The design of healthcare facilities is governed by many regulations and technical requirements. It is also affected by many less defined needs and pressures. Among the most pressing of these are the need to support the patient families' presence and participation in healthcare delivery. Therefore, to achieve such a hospital ward setting that is patient and family centred careful assessment of family care actions and transaction spaces is required. This can be accomplished by employing strategies and tactics that stimulate and explore the research framework from data collection to analysis in line with the goal of the research. Several tactics can be employed to examine the hospital ward spaces and family care actions towards a sustainable inpatient setting that is conscious of various patient and family attributes. Consequently, this chapter presents five multiple strategies that was combined to elicit information required in guiding a design process that eventually create a sustainable inpatient setting that is conscious of family actions.

Methodological Approaches in Designing Healthcare Setting

The ever-increasing healthcare staff requirement for a conducive working environment is perplexing. In addition, the expectations of the patients' and their families for the very best available medical and nursing care in a healing environment is becoming more challenging, hence the need for contemporary, valid and reliable research in modern healthcare practice. In achieving this, several perplexing research methods and approaches that are either quantitative or qualitative can be employed by healthcare researchers. While quantitative research is good at generalizing about large groups, qualitative research provides a level of descriptive detail and depth that is impossible to achieve quantitatively. Thus, qualitative research is a more agreeable method for studying *how* and *why* individuals interact within social contexts (Patton, 1990). Prominent among qualitative methods are observation, interview, action research, focus group, ethnography, illuminative case studies, phenomenology and historical analysis (Basset, 2004). However, the suitability of a method depends on the nature of the study. There are quite a number of studies that investigated the significance of humanising and improving health care and healthcare environments in order to increase users' wellbeing in the fields of nursing (Aiken *et al.*, 2012; Laura, 2006), medicine (Sadatsafavi *et al.*, 2013), human psychology (Grauman, 2002) and recently architecture (Devlin and Arneill, 2003; Dijkstra *et al*, 2006; Hendrich, 2003; Heyland and Tranmer, 2001; Lawson, 2005, 2013). Similarly, several strategies for identifying family needs in healthcare settings are found in the fields of psychiatry (Dixon et al., 2001), paediatric (Kuo *et al.,* 2012), dementia (Ter Meulen and Wright, 2012), elderly (Nayeri, *et al,* 2013) and intensive care unit (Johnson, Abraham, and Parrish, 2004). Yet, there are tactics used in investigating the relationship between healthcare environment, healthcare outcome and patient's satisfaction (Devlin and Arneill, 2003; Khalaila, 2013; O'Connor *et al.,* 2012; Ulrich, 2000).

Such methodological strategies used for research in healthcare setting suggest a varied and multidimensional approach that depends on the discipline and purpose of the study. Thus, different frameworks evolve in stimulating new research, investigating multidimensionality, creating operational definitions that assist in achieving a safe and healthy environment for both staff, patients and their families (Ampt *et al.,* 2008). Methodologies mostly applied in healthcare environment research are mostly of case study approach because of its ability to allow for exploration and understanding of complex issues in their natural setting. Case study has been described by Yin (2003) as an empirical investigation of a contemporary phenomenon within its natural context, especially when there are no clear boundaries between the phenomenon and the context (Hyett *et al.*, 2014; Nord, 2003). For instance, it was used in investigating patients' safety in a hospital ward (Hignett and Lu, 2010). In addition, it is often used by researchers in the field of built environment such as studying privacy in a hospital (Alalouch 2009), restorative environment for children (Said, 2006), relationship between healthcare environment and healthcare outcome (Abbas and Ghazali, 2012; Devlin and Arneill, 2003; Dijkstra *et al.*, 2006; O'Connor *et al.*, 2012; Ulrich *et al.*, 2004) among others. Even though, there are other various research methods being employed in eliciting perceptions and experience relevant to person-environment studies. Most common among them is interview, survey, concept review (Åstedt-Kurki *et al.*, 2001; Aiken et al., 2012), and theory development (Patton, 1990). However, there is a significant increase in the body of scholarship that supports a case study approach especially in a healthcare setting for its ability to portray the richness in social relations, use of and attitude to space and as well discovering underlying values and meanings (Nord, 2003). Consequently, this research approach implies a contextual relationship with physical space of a hospital ward and the routine action and interaction of the patients and their families. Therefore, this method is importantly recommended since there is no clear evident boundary between the familial caregiving and the hospital ward setting.

Charting the Philosophical Stance

Research quality can be improved when inclined to philosophical assumptions. Paradigms are used in describing different approaches to research. Studies are situated within a frame of assumptions which Denzin and Lincoln (2008) called paradigm. They are referred to as systems of inquiry with the explicit level of study's ontological assumptions that depend on the nature of the research (Groat and Wang, 2002). The epistemology of a study according to Creswell (2012) is the determinant of its theory base and most suitable guide towards attaining research method. Studies of this type are structured between the objective and subjective approaches that adopt epistemological knowledge position of interpretative paradigm.

Considering the nature of this study, it requires to be rooted in a research paradigm that seeks to explore contextual social and cultural phenomena in a setting (Caplan and Van Harrison, 1993), in which people-environment (PE) relationship is viewed as that world, as it is lived in and experienced, within which humans perceive, act and of which they belong (Grauman, 2002). As such the procedures to be used here are inductive in nature as they are based on the researcher's own experience in collection and analysis of data. The textual data from field notes and transcribed interview, as well as the photographs and the graphical representation need to be condensed into themes, categories and domains (Patton, 1990). Subsequently, the data could develop into an in-depth knowledge of the actions and interactions of patients' family within the hospital ward spaces. This basic assumption that guided the research inquiries, composition of the research questions and inference suggested pragmatic approach as most appropriate. The essence of this approach is not only to seek a truth that is not independent of human experience, but rather to also achieve better and richer experience through scientific analysis, artistic exploration, social negotiation, or any combination of these different approaches (Yardley and Bishop, 2008).

The Investigation Trails

In healthcare design, qualitative research has proven to be a valuable method in exploring how healthcare environments can be enhanced for an improved outcome to those receiving and providing care (Malagon-Maldonado, 2014; Choi and Bosch, 2013). It became popular in healthcare research for being the only way to fully examine how and why individuals interact within certain social or cultural contexts (Patton, 2014). Considering the static nature of social contexts been studied, its investigation under natural setting will be difficult using other research techniques. Qualitative researchers study culture because they believe that knowledge is created through social interaction with others. Of course, this knowledge can change as societies and cultures change. Studying other cultures then becomes one way of discovering new knowledge. Because it provides most of the grounded information required for evidence-based design. Moreover, in this type of research where the purpose is to study actions and interactions of the patient's family within the hospital ward spaces, a better understanding of the phenomenon in relation to their transaction spaces is required. It also involves identifying the perceptual responses of healthcare personnel on such action and interactions rather than to generalize to a larger population.

Therefore, the initial approach in this context is to base the inquiry on research questions because they are considered as the major concern of a qualitative inquiry (Bendassolli, 2013). In order to deal with this situation sensibly and realistically besides the practical rather than theoretical considerations, a mixed method is deemed suitable due to its ability to provide a better understanding of a phenomenon (Creswell, 2012). Precisely the use of an exploratory sequential research design suffices. The process initially requires a suitable case to be identified. It can be achieved by using criteria that justifies the site selection. Qualitative research provides that the researcher be sensitive to the context of the research for the fact that the data and findings are context specific, which may or may not have any generalizability to other settings or context (Malagon-Maldonado, 2014).

Afterwards, exploration of the familial caregiving concept is required in order to identify the typology of family care actions and interactions. This can be achieved through an exploratory survey using an interview and subsequently, an in-depth study using observation techniques. For triangulation, use of survey questionnaires and a brainstorming session known as design charrette can provide the data required in explaining the relationship found in the qualitative data (Morse, 1991). Subsequently, the principles of behavioural mapping and scrutiny of architectural drawings are very suitable techniques for examining the space activity relationship. In all, the use of multiple methods in the elicitation of information about familial caregiving does provide sufficient data required for analysis, evaluation and conclusion.

1. Interactive Approach

The exploratory survey provides first-hand insight of the familial caregiving phenomena in a hospital ward setting. The direct interaction with the respondent through interview is believed to provide an in-depth understanding of social phenomena in such research and is useful in exploring the views, experiences, beliefs of individuals on specific matters (Åstedt-Kurki et al., 2001). Interviews are as well considered most appropriate in this situation where little is known about the study phenomenon or where detailed insights are required from individual participants (Denzin & Lincoln, 2008). Therefore, interviewing the patients does reveal the extent and nature of family participation in caregiving. As such an unstructured interview was conducted with a certain number of patients in order to elicit their understanding and perception of the concept of familial caregiving by asking questions on the need for familial caregiving. The codes and themes generated from these responses at this stage thereafter guided the formulation of the research design.

2. Surveillance Strategy

One of the famous qualitative methods of inquiry is surveillance of research milieu through observation. It involves a direct description of actions and interactions of specific social groups obtained through observation and verbal communication as they happen naturally (Geest and Finkler, 2004). Observation differs depending on the observer's degree of participation or involvement in the scene. In this situation, this kind of study has to follow an opportunistic sampling pattern where the researcher has the liberty to decide the activity to observe, which people to observe and to interview and the time frame selected to collect the data (Patton, 2002).

The procedure requires a field observation to be carried out more than once (Patton, 2002) on dual purpose. Firstly, there is need to study the typology of family care actions, then the space activity relationship. It can be limited to a number of rounds when the data obtained in subsequent rounds is not different from the earlier rounds, hence, indication of data saturation (Patton, 2014). Each round of twelve hours should comprise of three shifts in each of the wards in the hospital where observation is to be scheduled in eight hours per shift over three consecutive days in a ward. A similar schedule is to be repeated in another ward to observe similarities and differences and as a pair wise comparison (Elo et al., 2014). Furthermore, the routine in the second and third round is to be repeated after two weeks from the earlier round when the researcher assumes that most of the patients previously observed might have been discharged. In all, this would give a total of eighteen sessions to be conducted in typical wards. The intention of the morning session is to observe the early morning, pre-ward round and ward round activities while the afternoon session is to capture the post-ward round activities, meals and other related activities whereas the night session will observe the overnight activities.

3. Survey Questionnaire

The third strategy useful in studying the perception toward the attributes of familial caregiving is quantitative in nature. There is an outstanding tradition in social science research methods that promotes the use of multiple methods. This form of research approach is usually termed as convergent methodology, multi-method/multi-trait, convergent validation or, what is known as triangulation (Leech, 2007; Yardley and Bishop, 2008). These various notions are all of the opinion that qualitative and quantitative methods should be seen as complementary rather than as opposite opinions. In the context of this study, sequential triangulation (Morse, 1991) strategy was recommended where the quantitative aspect of the study was designed to elicit the perception of the healthcare personnel and the patient's family on the attributes of familial caregiving identified qualitatively. Sequential triangulation strategy is usually employed if the findings of one method are essential for planning the next method (Morse, 1991). The survey questionnaire employed here was to measure the effect of the cultural attributes and poor hospital ward operations in promoting the familial caregiving practices. The Survey questionnaire was designed with items grouped under the categories developed based on the domains of the qualitative study findings. The items contained in the survey questionnaire formed the parameters constructed based on the themes generated from the observation. The findings from this inquiry, apart from eliciting the opinion of the end users of the facility, ultimately revealed the magnitude of the factors so measured.

4. Document Scrutiny

To have a better understanding of the hospital ward configuration and facilities which is the research milieu requires the study of the architectural drawings using content analysis. The content analysis of floor plans of the hospital ward setting provided the meaning and information embedded in graphical representation or visual communication messages (Cole 1988). This method is famous in the fields of communication, journalism, sociology, psychology and business for analysing hymns, newspaper and magazine articles, advertisements and political speeches (Elo et al., 2014). The content analysis of the drawings revealed the details of the spatial components and organisation that guided the behavioural mapping.

5. Behavioural mapping

This kind of study requires a location based investigation that studies human behaviour and activities by use of annotation on maps, plans, videos and photographs either manually or digitally (Chosco *et al.*, 2010). Behavioural Mapping referred to circumstances where peoples' activities, behaviours, characteristics and movements are directly observed and systematically recorded in time and space (Chosco *et al.*, 2010). Being a non-intrusive direct observational method, it is found suitable for use in understanding the behavioural dynamics of a built environment (Choi and Bosch, 2013). Behavioural mapping is useful in identifying environmental affordances and particular design practices for the fact that it records the precise location of people and their activities on floor plans instead of categorised locations. Even though, this method is popular in the study of children's outdoor activities (Choi and Bosch, 2013; Chosco *et al.*, 2010). However, it has also been used in different healthcare environments, including research on the use of gardens in a paediatric hospital (Said, 2006), school children in a playground and a study on resident behaviour at a nursing station of a senior facility (Shepley, n.d.).

Principles of behavioural mapping are employed mainly in three types of applied research (Shepley, n.d.). The first is during a pre-occupancy evaluation research intended to inform the programming process. The second is in post-occupancy evaluation which is intended to confirm designed goals achievements, while the third is to examine innovative design prototypes in order to confirm their appropriateness. Examining how appropriately hospital ward facilities afford familial caregiving thus falls into the third category. In this kind of research with interest in the interaction of patient's family and hospital spaces, location for actions and interactions of the patient's family could be recorded manually on the floor plan and the frequency of such occurrences recorded as field notes in all the wards studied.

During an observation sweep or round, the observer conversant with the behavioural mapping, walks around a unit in a predetermined way that allows for visual inspection of every bedside, corridors, foyers, courtyards and conveniences. The researcher needs to adopt place-centred instantaneous scans (Design Methods, 2014), considered as, the principal method of behavioural mapping. It is the least invasive approach (Lehrner, 1979) where the observer sets intervals of one minute, quickly notes people's activity within a certain area and moves on to other areas. These scans have been observed to be less offensive than continuous observation. On such occasions, the researcher comes around, take field notes and ask questions necessary to aid better understanding of the situation (Loflan and Loflan, 1995). Furthermore, patients or patients' family may be asked questions in order to elicit more information on certain action or interaction observed during the observation sessions. This sandwich (concurrent observation and interview) approach gives the observer the opportunity to explore the internal state of scenes or person being observed for validation purpose and crosschecking of findings (Patton, 2002). Considering these momentary scans for this study, interobserver reliability was inherently achieved thereby providing systematic samples of familial caregiving activities and space-activity relationship patterns.

6. Design Charrette

To successfully achieve a sustainable family conscious inpatient setting where all stakeholders are satisfied with the end product, a collaboration across design team and professionals from healthcare disciplines is essential (Fong, 2003). The significance of multidisciplinary teams' collaboration is not only limited to improvement in product and facility design, but is also essential in knowledge creation and sharing among teams thereby leading to a more productive outcome (Knox, 2013).

The most commonly used method in increasing collaboration and communication across disciplines is the charrette (Knox, 2013). Charrette is a design-based, accelerated, collaborative brainstorming session carried out during the design period (Suba, 2011). Charrette involves the use of multidisciplinary teams to assist and enhance knowledge creation and sharing among participants through interacting and communicating with one another in identifying and solving problems (Fong, 2003). In this context, principles of charrette were employed in organising brainstorming session by the researcher and attended by professionals nominated by their respective professional bodies. The major reason is to have consensus opinion of the design and healthcare professionals on the design implication in providing for familial caregiving in the hospital wards. Conducting a successful charrette session involves adequate planning, mobilisation and conducting the session.

The planning of the charrette requires setting up a steering committee by the researcher to assist in guiding the planning process, discussing and assessing the objectives and logistic issues, thus seeking for support from key individuals and organizations (Design charrette, n.d.). The committee as well should agree on the number of representatives from each of the organisations. Subsequently, invitation letters for participation are to be sent to the secretariats of the prospective organisations. There is need for several follow-ups in order to get their responses. All the nominees are to be contacted personally, briefed on the purpose of the session and their interest sought. For those that may decline for various reasons, they should suggest a replacement who should also be contacted later. The committee should also secure a befitting venue for the programme.

The programme facilitated by a chairman is usually to be broken down into three sessions; the preliminary, the breakout and the concluding sessions. The preliminary session starts with the introduction of the programme by the researcher where the highlight of the study and the expected outcome of the programme is presented. The preliminary session needs to feature paper presentation focussing on the subject matter. Thereafter, some of the professional bodies among the healthcare personnel could be asked to share their personal experience on activities of patients' family in hospital wards stating particularly the good side of their engagement and the challenges as well.

Subsequently, the session under the guidance of the facilitator should design and adopt a framework and mode of operation (*modus operandi*) that would guide the breakout session. After a tea break, the breakout sessions continue with each of the professionals forming a group to deliberate on the subject matter based on the modus operandi and come up with their consensus opinion after which the final part of the session would be reconvened. During the final part of the session, each group reports back to the general assembly, where their recommendations are presented and either adopted by the house, modified or discarded. Finally, the house adopts a consensus opinion on the implication of family inclusion and the designing of hospital ward with familial caregiving.

The documentation of the whole session could be captured using audio, video and photographs taken concurrently. Discussion during the breakout sessions by each of the group should be recorded with audio tape. The summary of the session's outcome as captured and documented by the rapporteur should also be considered for further analysis. Consequently, at the final stage of this study a visioning charrette session which involved designers and end users of the healthcare facility was organised. The charrette session aided in identifying consensus opinion on the implications of providing for familial caregiving on hospital ward design.

Achieving a Sustainable Hospital Ward Setting

Scientific research is a systematic process of inquiry, and the focus is on gathering a multitude of information that culminates in an evidenced-based conclusion. This process of studying the concept of family and space so described could provide the detailed information required in making the decision for a sustainable family conscious hospital ward environment. The initial stage which involved interview and observation in the procedure unearthed the nature of the family actions and interactions toward caring for the hospitalised patient. It did not only uncover the type of care provided, but it also revealed the form and character by which the care is given. Ultimately, these procedures provided a better understanding of the subject matter for further evaluation.

By revealing the end users' opinions about the facility toward family involvement in care, the subsequent quantitative approach provided a way of all-inclusive method that allowed for user participation. The rigorous process, from developing the instrument, validation and administration, as well as analysis of the data so obtained, provided the information required in answering the related research question or hypothesis.

As for the study of space and activity relationship, studying the spatial configuration of the hospital ward using the architectural drawing provided a better understanding of the research milieu. The information about the facilities, functions and functional relationship in the ward guided the process of behavioural mapping that eventually revealed the family transaction spaces. Furthermore, the behavioural mapping, being a famous method in the fields of urban planning for studying location based activities (Chosco et al., 2010), its principles and application is not limited to the revelation of space requiring design attention, but also revealed in this study, the extent to which such spaces are used. Adequate observations using the principles of behavioural mapping revealed significant information on the family's interaction with the hospital ward spaces and their preferences that are essential in architectural design. Conclusively, the consensus opinion on the implications of providing for familial caregiving on hospital ward design was decided during the charrette session and remains a valuable input from the stakeholders in healthcare delivery and healthcare environment design. The principles of charrette employed in this strategy provided a convenient way by which the stakeholders gave useful suggestions and information required in achieving the required goal which could not be obtained through other methods.

The combination of these six strategies in the investigation of patient and family relationship has demonstrated that various methods used in different fields of study can fuse together towards building a framework for another scientific inquiry. The sequential and parallel order by which the investigation was scheduled shows some rigour in the approach used for data elicitation. Most importantly, the findings from such rigorous process are believed to be very sound because of its high validity and reliability (Golafshani, 2003).

Conclusion

The layout of procedures described in this process of inquiry is based on the principles of case study approach. Following these procedures should lead to a finding that is not only evidence based but to also show all-inclusiveness in the information obtained from different perspectives. The strategies explained here in understanding the concept of family caregiving and space activity relationship are useful not only to the designers of the healthcare environment, but also to the healthcare providers. The triangulation of such strategies ultimately improved the validity of the outcome and reliability of the findings. Furthermore, the underpinning and detailed description of these procedures suggest that they can be applied in different disciplines for studies in different research environments and for various research purposes.

References

Abbas, M. Y., & Ghazali, R. (2012). Healing Environment: Paediatric Wards – Status and Design Trend. *Procedia - Social and Behavioural Sciences, 49,* 28–38.

Aiken, L. H., Sermeus, W., Van den Heede, K., Sloane, D. M., Busse, R., McKee, M. Kutney-Lee, A. (2012). Patient safety, satisfaction, and quality of hospital care: cross sectional surveys of nurses and patients in 12 countries in Europe and the United States. *BMJ, 344.*

Ampt, A., Harris, P., & Maxwell, M. (2008). *The health impacts of the design of hospital facilities on patient recovery and wellbeing, and staff wellbeing: A review of the literature.* Liverpool, NSW, Australia: Centre for Primary Health Care and Equity.

Åstedt-Kurki, P., Paavilainen, E., & Lehti, K. (2001). Methodological issues in interviewing families in family nursing research. *Journal of Advanced Nursing, 35*(2), 288–293.

Basset, C. (2004). *Qualitative Research in Health Care.* London N1 2UN England: Whurr Publishers Ltd.

Bendassolli, P. F. (2013). Theory Building in Qualitative Research: Reconsidering the Problem of Induction. *Forum Qualitative Sozialforschung / Forum: Qualitative Social Research, 14*(1). Retrieved from http://www.qualitative-research.net/index.php/fqs/article/view/1851

Caplan, R. D., & Van Harrison, R. (1993). Person-Environment Fit Theory: Some History, Recent Developments, and Future Directions. *Journal of Social Issues, 49*(4), 253–275.

Choi, Y.-S., & Bosch, S. J. (2013). Environmental affordances: designing for family presence and involvement in patient care. *Health Environments Research and Design Journal, 6*(4), 53–75.

Chosco, N. G., Moor, R. C., & Islam, M. Z. (2010). Behaviour Mapping: A Method for Linking Preschool Physical Activity and Outdoor Design. *Medicine and Science in Sports and Exercise*, 513–519.

Creswell, J. W. (2012). *Educational Research: Planning, Conducting and evaluating Quantitative and Qualitative Research* (4th ed.). Boston, USA: Pearson.

Denzin, N. K., & Lincoln, S. Y. (2008). *Strategies of Qualitative inquiry* (2nd ed.). USA: SAGE Publications.

Design charrette: A vehicle for consultation or collaboration. (n.d.). Retrieved 20 June 2013, from http://www.academia.edu/1277880/Design_charrette_A_vehicle_ forconsultation orcollaboration

Design Methods. (2014). Retrieved from http://www.doctordisruption.com/design/design-methods-24-behavioural-mapping

Devlin, S. A., & Arneill, A. B. (2003). Healthcare Environments and Patient Outcomes: A Review of the Literature. *Environment and Behaviour, 35*(5), 665–695.

Dijkstra, K., Pieterse, M., & Pruyn, A. (2006). Physical environmental stimuli that turn healthcare facilities into healing environments through psychologically mediated effects: systematic review. *Journal of Advanced Nursing, 56*(2), 166–181.

Dixon, L., McFarlane, W. R., Lefley, H., Lucksted, A., Cohen, M., Falloon, I., … Sondheimer, D. (2001). Evidence-Based Practices for Services to Families of People With Psychiatric Disabilities. *Psychiatric Services, 52*(7), 903–910.

Elo, S., Kääriäinen, M., Kanste, O., Pölkki, T., Utriainen, K., & Kyngäs, H. (2014). Qualitative Content Analysis A Focus on Trustworthiness. *SAGE Open, 4*(1).

Fong, P. S. W. (2003). Knowledge creation in Multidisciplinary project teams: An empirical study of the processes and their dynamic interrelationships. *International Journal of Project Management, 21*(7), 479–486.

Geest, S. van der, & Finkler, K. (2004). Hospital ethnography: introduction. *Social Science & Medicine, 59*, 1995–2001.

Golafshani, N. (2003). Understanding Reliability and Validity in Qualitative Research. *The Qualitative Report, 8*(4), 597–607.

Grauman, C. F. (2002). The Phenomenological Approach to People-Environment Studies. In *Handbook of Environmental Psychology* (pp. 95–113). New York, NY, USA: John Wiley & Sons, Inc.

Hendrich, A. (2003). Optimizing physical space for improved outcomes: Satisfaction and the bottom line. In *Proceedings of Minicourse* (Vol. 76). Atlanta, Georgia: Institute for Healthcare Improvement & The Center for Healthcare Design.

Heyland, D. K., & Tranmer, J. E. (2001). Measuring family satisfaction with care in the intensive care unit: The development of a questionnaire and preliminary results. *Journal of Critical Care, 16*(4), 142–149.

Hignett, S., & Lu, J. (2010). Space to care and treat safely in acute hospitals: Recommendations from 1866 to 2008. *Applied Ergonomics, 41*(5), 666–673.

Hyett, N., Kenny, A., & Virginia, D.-S. (2014). Methodology or method? A critical review of qualitative case study reports. *International Journal of Qualitative Studies on Health and Well-Being,* 9 doi: 10.3402/qhw.v9.23606.

Johnson, B. H., Abraham, M. R., & Parrish, R. N. (2004). Designing the neonatal intensive care unit for optimal family involvement. *Clinics in Perinatology, 31*(2), 353–382.

Khalaila, R. (2013). Patients' family satisfaction with needs met at the medical intensive care unit. *Journal of Advanced Nursing, 69*(5), 1172–1182.

Knox, M. W. (2013). *Impact Of Charrettes And Their Characteristics On Achieved Leed Certification* (MSc). Colorado State University, Fort Collins, Colorado.

Kuo, Z., Houtrow, A. J., Arango, P., Kuhlthau, K. A., Simons, J. M., & John, N. M. (2012). Family Centered Care: Current Applications and Future Directions in Paediatric Healthcare. *Maternal Child Health, 16,* 297–305.

Laura, L. (2006, March 22). New standards for Hospital call for Patient to get Private room. *The Wall Street Journal.*

Lawson, B. (2005). Evidence based Design for Health. Hospital Engineering and Facilities Management. Retrieved from http://www.hfmsnj.org

Lawson, B. (2013). Design and the Evidence. *Procedia - Social and Behavioural Sciences, 105,* 30–37.

Leech, N. L. (2007). An Array of qualitative data analysis tools: A call for Data analysis Triangulation. *School Psychology Quarterly, 22*(4), 577–584.

Lehrner, P. N. (1979). *Handbook of ethological methods.* New York, NY, USA: Garland STMP.

Lincoln, S. Y., & Guba, E. G. (1985). *Naturalistic Inquiry.* Thousand Oaks: SAGE.

Loflan, J., & Loflan, H. (1995). *Analyzing social settings: A Guide to Qualitative observation and analysis.* Belmont C.A.: Wadsworth.

Malagon-Maldonado, G. (2014). Qualitative Research in Health Design. *HERD : Health Environments Research & Design Journal, 7*(4), 120–134.

Morse, J. M. (1991). Approaches to Qualitative-Quantitative Methodological Triangulation. *Nursing Research, 40*(2), 120–123.

Nayeri, N. D., Gholizadeh, L., Mohammadi, E., & Yazdi, K. (2013). Family Involvement in the Care of Hospitalized Elderly Patients. *Journal of Applied Gerontology,*

Nord, C. (2003). *The Visible Patient: Hybridity and inpatient ward design in Namibian Context.* Stockholm: Royal Institute of Technology.

O'Connor, M., O'Brien, A., Bloomer, M., Morphett, J., Peters, L., Hall, H., ... Munro, I. (2012). The Environment of Inpatient Healthcare Delivery and Its Influence on the Outcome of Care. *HERD : Health Environments Research & Design Journal, 6*(1), 104–16.

Patton, M. Q. (1990). *Qualitative evaluation and research methods* (2nd ed.). California: SAGE.

Patton, M. Q. (2002). *Qualitative research and evaluation methods* (3rd ed.). Thousand Oaks: SAGE.

Patton, M. Q. (2014). *Qualitative Research and Evaluation Methods: Integrating Theory and Practice.* Sage Publications: UK.

Sadatsafavi, H., Walewski, J., & Shepley, M. M. (2013). Factors influencing evaluation of patient areas, work spaces, and staff areas by healthcare professionals. *Indoor and Built Environment.*

Said, I. (2006). *Garden Restorative Environment for Children in Malaysian Hospitals* (PhD thesis). Universiti Teknologi Malaysia, Johor Bahru, Malaysia.

Shepley, M. M. (n.d.). *Family Behaviour in a Single-Family Room NICU* (AIA Report on University Research No. 5). American Institute of Architects.

Suba, L. (2011). When Is a Charrette Session Useful? Retrieved 1 December 2014, from http://www.brighthubpm.com/project-planning/123216-using-charrettes-in-the-project-planning-phases/

Ter Meulen, R., & Wright, K. (2012). Family Solidarity and Informal Care: The Case of Care for People with Dementia. *Bioethics, 26*(7), 361–368.

Ulrich, R. (2000). Evidence based environmental design for improving medical outcomes. In *Healing By Design* (Vol. 3, pp. 1–3). Montreal, Canada: McGill University Health Centre.

Ulrich, R., Xiaobo, Q., Craig, Z., Anjali, J., & Ruchi, C. (2004). Role of the Physical Environment in the Hospital of the 21st century.

Yardley, L., & Bishop, F. (2008). Mixing Qualitative and Quantitative Methods: A Pragmatic Approach. In *The SAGE Handbook of Qualitative Research in Psychology* (pp. 352–371), UK: SAGE Publications Ltd.

Yin, R. K. (2003). *Case study research: Design and methods* (3rd). Southern Oaks, Califonia: SAGE.

Chapter 5

Analytical strategy for measuring users' behaviour in sustainable housing research

Abubakar Danladi Isah

Department of Architecture,
Federal University of Technology Minna, Nigeria

arcmuzaifa@futminna.edu.ng

Abstract:

Introduction - This chapter describes a research design structure that highlights the paradigm, theory, method, strategies and tactics applied to inspire and explore housing research. Inclusively, it covers data gathering to findings in concurrence with sustainable development principles.

Purpose - The goal is basically targeted towards creating housing research procedure that focuses on core values in the spatial organisation of cultured dwelling units in urban locales. It centres on the understanding of activities and activity-space relationships of housing inhabitants particularly in culture sensitive societies. A link which suggests that users' behaviour reveals cultural attributes in space use that could facilitate design thoughts.

Design / Methodology / Approach - Systematically, Groat and Wang (2002)'s research process that highlighted four major hierarchical components of paradigm, theory, method and techniques was used to project the concept described in this study. In a sequential arrangement, the components considered suggested suitable research philosophical paradigm then proceeded to argue on the theoretical basis in order to define appropriate analytical traits of sustainable housing research phenomenon. Thereafter, techniques and tactics that could guide data collection and data processing with a focus on the users were established while delineating validity and reliability strategies for authenticating possible outcomes.

Findings - At the end, this research discovered an effective scientific system of inquiry - linking paradigm with theoretical underpining comprising of established seminal theories that include culture specificity of the built environment in Man Environment Relations (Rapoport, 1983). Others are Environment Behaviour Relations (Rapoport, 2000); the user centred theory of the built environment (Vischer, 2008) and the cultural paradigm related to the Etic and Emic theory of cross cultural research. After which the choice of ethnographic principles in the search for sustainable housing attributes was recommended as an appropriate strategy suitable for sustainable housing research enquiry. Ethnography was projected to explicitly provide the culture constituents [values, needs and desires] that influence user initiated interactions with space towards users' housing satisfaction. Therefore, it provides researchers with a choice of suitable method to be adopted for sustainable housing research.

Practical implication - In ensuring the validity and reliability of housing study towards sustainable urban development in tune with United Nations' (UN) guidelines, the emerging research design, operationalized research process, parameters and variables are usually user and context sensitive. This chapter thus provides a direction to be explored systematically within the established research framework in examining such phenomenon.

Originality/value - This chapter contributes towards directing sustainable housing research procedures which are no longer devoid of users' mainstream socio-cultural values and behavioural functions.

Keywords: Housing research, Sustainable development, Mainstream values, Culture, Behavioural Studies.

Introduction

As obtainable in any research voyage, setting the research process within scientifically proven domain increases its credibility, believability and trustworthiness, while authenticating the evidence in its outcome. Housing research methods require absolute credibility, validity and reliability that centre around the stakeholders particularly the end users. Thus, a research procedure that assures these research attributes should be essentially sorted in achieving sustainable housing research. Accordingly, the study opted for Groat and Wang (2002)'s research process that consists of four major hierarchical components- paradigm, theory, methods and techniques in promoting sustainable housing research strategy. In the process, a research procedure which reflects mainstream values in spatial configurations of sustainable housing research is revealed. The evolving methodological strategy first sequentially position sustainable housing research in suitable philosophical paradigm in order to identify the principles that direct its knowledge extension process, towards seeking solutions to housing research as a phenomenon being examined (Fellows and Liu, 2009). Thereafter, theories- a set of suggestions describing various traits of the phenomenon as explained by Berg and Lune, (2004) evolves to strengthen the research foundation and focus. Thus, relying on philosophical underpinning for validity and consistency, theory building hypothesised explicitly the descriptions about the natural features and socio-cultural world that would lead to findings which are subjected to and verifiable by the scientific process of research inquiry.

Additionally, in order to articulate the knowledge gap and research direction and also establish the research focus, first there is the need to hinge research on a recognised methodological framework. This is usually evident in the epistemological and ontological perspectives of the research. Groat and Wang's (2002), epistemological research picture shown in Figure 5.1 is considered appropriate as a methodological structure.

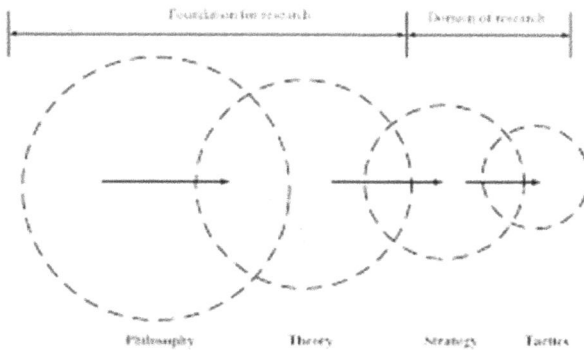

Figure 5.1 Methodological Research Structure
Source: Groat and Wang, (2002)

Philosophical Stance for Sustainable Housing Research

Social, economic and physical dimensions in housing research are proportionate to UN's indices of sustainable development in urban growth and renewal particularly with regards to sustainable housing and urban development. Essentially, philosophical approach suitable in relating the indices of these dimensions is usually subjective because housing attributes as defined by UN for sustainable development are focused on environmental quality. As such the philosophical standpoint in sustainable housing research should be directed towards qualitative realm in both epistemology and ontology (knowledge and nature).

Apposite Research Metaphysical Paradigm

Scientists postulate studies within structured assumptions known as paradigms (Denzin and Lincoln, 2008) or system of inquiry (Groat and Wang, 2002) which clearly relates the study's ontological assumptions (nature of reality) that is a subject of the research nature. Similarly, it relates the study's epistemology (nature of knowledge) that defines its theory base as well as the appropriate research strategy (Willig, 2001). Therefore, since sustainable housing research is phenomenological in nature where salient issues of social lifestyles are to be examined, interpreted and reflected in the design, then emancipatory and interpretive paradigms are most appropriate. Consequently, sustainable housing research should be structured in between the two extremes of objective and subjective approaches, adopting the epistemological knowledge position of emancipatory and phenomenological/interpretive paradigms. This is because epistemological position assumes the subject knowledge as a reflection of contextual field information and human projections which in this case is about the social phenomena of housing and its liveability. Indeed, the social phenomena of housing positions its philosophical knowledge and bond housing research with appropriate methods being employed. Surely, philosophical knowledge tends to be beneficial in understanding the basic concepts and background assumptions of these methods.

As a result, housing phenomenological research work like any research engagement should stem from an appropriate system of enquiry. The goal of focusing on exploring socio-cultural factors that influence occupants' liveability in housing such as layout transformation leads to the understanding of the role of cultural traits and its significance in housing consumption. In essence, design considerations should advance from people's interaction with spaces aptly referred to as users' behaviour. This paradigm centres on the occupants' interactive experiences with their dwellings over time adjusting to satisfy preferences and changing needs.

Evidently, this phenomenological approach recognizes several realities, assuming the impossibility of generalization in all situations but rather affirming that research design should originate from the researcher and the respondents' influence as outlined by Guba and Lincoln (1994) in (Groat and Wang, 2002). Likewise, historically situating sustainable housing research, taking into cognizance and emphasizing the indigenous content of settlements being investigated aligns it with the emancipatory paradigm. Furthermore, explicitly exposing unnoticed social, physical and cultural dynamics in the built environment aimed at transforming existing situation positions housing research in the sphere of emancipatory system of inquiry. Therefore, even though people think and act differently in space transactions, they usually have a common point of cognitive convergence that defines the group's behaviour as illustrated in Figure 5.2. Consequently, sustainable housing research fits into both emancipatory and phenomenological research paradigms as presented in Figure 5.3.

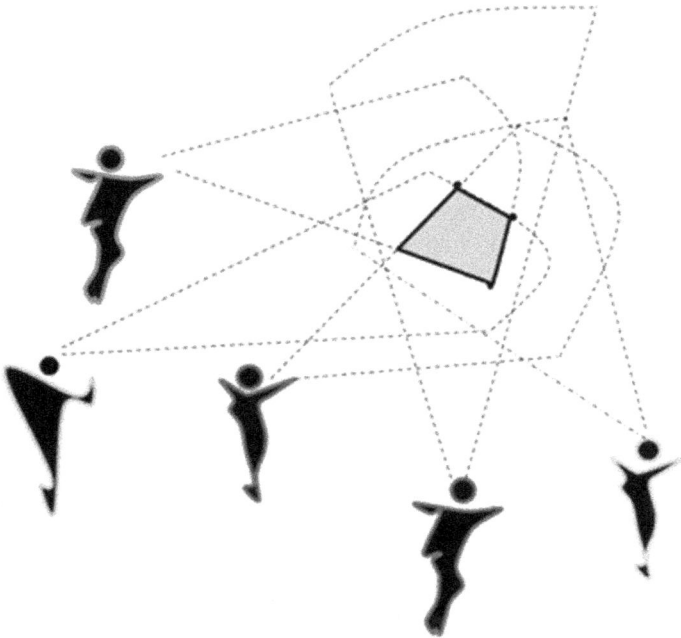

Figure 5.2 People's cognition with common converging point

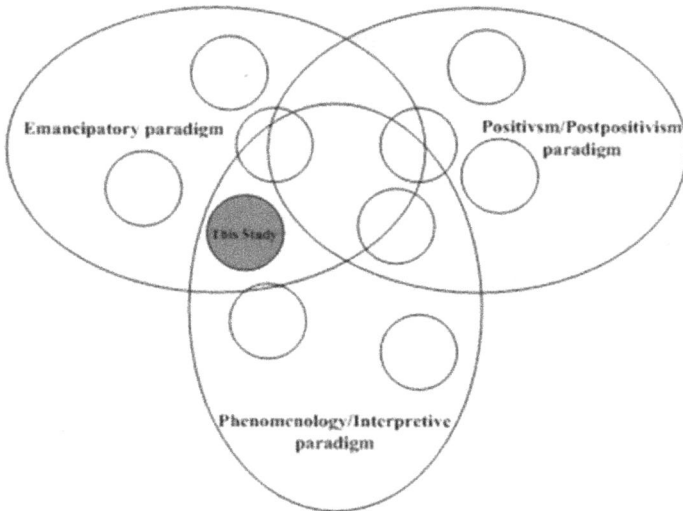

Figure 5.3 Clusters of systems of inquiry showing the location that fits sustainable housing research

Source Groat and Wang, (2002)

From the forgone, sustainable housing research focus is built on strong foot-
ings with epistemological assumptions defining the bigger picture of the
study. This implies that sustainable housing research which is rooted in
pragmatic approach integrates methods based on its paradigm. Because of
the epistemological influence exhibited in social science research (Morgan,
2007). Hence such study is structured in both domains of interpretive and
emancipatory paradigms of scientific system of enquiry. As a result, the research approach is interpretive and phenomenological as the research inves-
tigates salient issues of sustainable housing.

For instance, sustainable housing research such as "housing transformation" exploration reveals cultural tendencies of users which are deduced as
occupants' action on dwelling layout transactions. By this, households respond to their preferences and needs in adjusting dwellings as conceptual-
ized in housing adjustment theory (Morris and Winter, 1975). Also, various
contexts "culture-specificity" in design consideration sustained by explanatory
theory of environment-behaviour relation (EBR) of Rapoport, (2000) provides
socially sensitive architectural solutions to sustainable housing development.
Because it focuses housing research to particular contexts due to the subjectivity and diversification of human nature reflected in settlements and often
attributed to culture, environment and ethnic tendencies. Therefore, typical
housing phenomenon that assesses users' experience and focuses on culture
specific environment is elucidated through the bi-processes of phenomenological and interpretive systems of research enquiry. Again, this is because
these philosophical concepts are targeted at people's comprehension (human
behaviour) and interpretation of social settings (physical environment) as
affirmed by (Eriksson and Kovalainen, 2008).

Aligning Housing Attributes to Emancipatory Paradigm

Sustainable housing research aligns with the emancipatory paradigm, as
the later lay emphasis on the socio-cultural and ethnic subjects in the construction of reality while highlighting the historical and social situation of a
study's setting (Groat and Wang, 2002). Furthermore, it creates socially
valuable knowledge of precise historical and social settings on identified
salient phenomena (Oliver, 1992). Even though Oliver (1997) differs on the
idea of this methodology approach, opining that research is only adjudged
to be emancipatory simply after the research is conducted. However, the
emancipatory paradigm is applicable to various researches in numerous
fields. Thus, the focus and consideration of sustainable housing on social
backgrounds, exploring physical and cultural issues places it in the emancipatory domain of research inquiry.

Sustainable Housing Research: A Phenomenology

Phenomenology possesses the potential virtues of clarifying subjective experiences with concrete and broad articulation by emerging the researcher in the participants' experience, not without exposing researchers to the struggle of resolving enormous challenges particularly during the research process (Churchill,2006). Phenomenological paradigm equally focuses on specific phenomena, seeking to increase the perception and understanding of researchers on precise issues. Phenomenology is usually approached by means of qualitative methods. More so, while adopting qualitative method questionnaire survey and participant observation are strategies for soliciting information (Lester, 1999). The phenomenological paradigm connected with sustainability issues in housing such as housing transformation affords researchers with the observation of how participants interact with space over time as evidence for their expression of meanings to situations of interest (Starks and Trinidad, 2007). Adeptly taking to the fore participants' viewpoints with regards to the phenomenon (Lester, 1999). In this case, the viewpoint expressed relates to their experiences in the housing interaction process. Theoretically, the interpretive paradigm is engrained in phenomenology with both focused on structuring social reality (Berger and Luckmann, 1966). Therefore, it is recognised as an appropriate research paradigm for sustainable housing research.

Interpretive Attribute of Housing Research

An interpretive dimension enhances phenomenological research as a source of theory, policy and execution (Lester, 1999), believing in the researcher's interpretative cogency and the worth of the product - outcome (Teddlie, 2005). Interpretive paradigm strives for the comprehension of man-environment relations in culture specific settings. This is ensured through interpretive paradigm in order to develop a subjective meaning of one's action and experiences with the environment (Creswell, 2013).

Concisely, phenomenological and interpretive paradigms are appropriate for sustainable housing research meant to enhance and situate the empirical work historically within specific cultural context. Essentially, a phenomenological study seeks to understand the phenomena determined by contextual interpretation of researcher's observation and respondents' experience anticipated to activate cultural determinants for design thoughts in sustainable housing research. This is entrenched in the assumptions of the methods, thus strengthening existing links between research questions, participants, objectives and the study outcome.

For this purpose, it becomes appropriate to employ mixed method re-search design. As such, the quantitative method seems evidently easier to adopt in seeking data from households and dwelling occupants as it com-plements the overriding qualitative method of ethnographic studies in which participant observation is used to identify patterns resulting from users' interaction with housing spaces. Subsequently, information gathered through these varieties of sources could be subjected to both qualitative and statistical analysis such as ethnographic analysis, psychometric analy-sis and content analysis. Advantageously, a correlation of the findings from different sources through triangulation is likely to reveal the mainstream ideals for design considerations from the occupants' viewpoint that might offer design solutions. Beyond these, responsive housing design with sus-tainable developmental features evolve.

Analogical Inference in Achieving Suitable Research Method

In furtherance to the solidly laid philosophical stance and established theo-retical base in a typical sustainable housing research, the epistemological research domain echoes the research method. Subsequently, applicable strategy (method) and tactics (techniques) would stem from the theoretical composition of the research. Sustainable housing research tends towards qualitative perspective particularly in the context that deals with the inter-pretations of contemporary situations, emphasizing the researcher's role in the field as vital to the outcome. These are considered features of qualita-tive research (Groat and Wang, 2002). Since such study seeks to compre-hend a phenomenon with research questions focused on investigating so-cial and urban physical settings, it should be categorised as a case study research. Because qualitative research that involves field study in under-standing a social phenomenon adopts the case study strategy (Yin, 2014). The case study strategy remains tremendously widespread in social re-search, particularly when dealing with sets of specifically related ideas and preferences with in-depth inquiry in order to give the methodological pro-cess a detailed and distinctive character (Denscombe, 2007). Additionally, Woodside (2010) asserts that case study inquiries forecast, regulate and relate the understanding of groups and settings as well as families and cul-tures. Such empirical queries enable the understanding of the intricate social phenomenon that lies in real life situations (Yin, 2014). Hence, case study research aligns with research that tends towards discovery and syn-onymous with qualitative studies. Besides, multiple sites' study approach is considered appropriate in sustainable housing research that involves per-ceptions and thoughts of participants drawn from different backgrounds. This is to facilitate the development of common themes on spatial issues related to different indigenous settings. In addition, the case study approach if subjected to further detailed strategies could be regarded as mixed method approach in spite of existing overlaps (Khan, 2008). Thus, the inclusion of quantitative and qualitative information in sustainable housing research situates it in a mixed-mode research dimension.

Systematically, sustainable housing research better combines various settings as a result of diverse human and ethnic communalities while seeking the understanding of physical setting and inhabitants' behaviour. This operational methodology is a qualitative research that adopts multi-case studies strategy, with multi-phase sampling technique using mixed-method approach in data eliciting and processing as well as in the interpretation.

Investigative Tactics and Techniques

Afterwards, the understanding of the research process and path should be swiftly expatiated due to the need for further clarification and detailing the procedure as experienced while creating a research design. The research design explains the process of data collection, analysis and interpretation, in this situation by applying the mixed-method approach. Tactics and techniques involve specific instruction of explicit, compelling and prescribing character used to elaborate methods towards achieving specific goals by thinking and acting using instruments or/and tools in a systematic way within established rules and procedures (Jonker and Pennik, 2010). Essentially, research procedure sensibly, and successively link empirical data and research objectives to the conclusions (Yin, 2010). Thus, sequence and concurrency in explaining or exploring the operation are possible research procedural tactics in examining various objectives and relating the findings. Towards this realisation, undertaking an ethnographic study of communities comprising of indigenous groups should establish the core space use attributes in their housing layouts. Tactically, such investigative process should reflect both cultural and spatial tendencies sought in sustainable housing research which projects the liveability of inhabitants. Accordingly, this aligns with the benchmark for selection of technique(s) commonly used in such research inquiry which include; consideration of norms and criteria, personal preferences, context, principle of equifinality as well as internal and external developments as outlined by (Jonker and Pennink, 2010). The process thereby advances an outcome that directs development of design issues by providing a guide for future schemes. Advantageously, experts' validation of the outcome is another tactic that ensures believability and usability of findings while confirming the appropriateness in operationalization of the theories extended from the research framework.

In sum, sustainable housing research phenomenon could be investigated using a focused group observation, comparisons between traditional and urban housing provisions towards ensuring that users' demands are understood. Also, developing themes, statistical and qualitative queries followed by synthesis in establishing outcome are tactical approaches in extending an in-depth study. In this regard, the case study approach ensures focus on existing relationships and practises in social settings that are usually consistent and related (Denscombe, 2007).

Identifying Appropriate Methodological Framework

From the foregone, the framework of housing research could be developed based on the four components of epistemological research framework outlined by Groat and Wang (2002). This methodological framework is considered effective in directing sustainable housing research because it elaborates on the philosophical and theoretical dimensions as well as the appropriate method. The research design further outlines the strategies employed in the research domain.

Furthermore, it relates numerous tactics that enhance research quality even though it is optional as not all qualitative studies employ several strategies. However, combined strategies where multiple research approaches are adopted using multiple sources of data gathering and multiple analytic procedures enrich the sustainable solutions in housing research. These are the strengths of case study strategy as it invites, encourages and permit researchers to use a variety of sources, types of data and a range of methods in investigating a phenomenon (Denscombe, 2007). It thus fits the circumstances and specific needs of sustainable housing research. Above all, this procedure could better be pictorially and intensely shown graphically describing the step by step practices performed towards establishing the research goal. The typical research design that pictorially displays this methodological process is shown in Table 5.1.

In addition, meta-synthesis tactically clarify and aids the understanding of a phenomenon by creating a whole concept from its essentials (Walsh and Downe, 2005). Besides, an analytic evaluation of literature reinforces established findings of the subject towards instituting the theoretical framework that places the research gap. Qualitatively interpretive procedure enhances the explicit sense of the subject matter (Erwin *et al.*, 2011). Similarly, convergent parallel design consists of parallel data gathering where quantitative data could be embedded in a predominant qualitative data that explains the phenomenon (Creswell, 2012). Impliedly, the outcome of one objective most likely determines the consideration of a subsequent objective in sequence. Ethnography could be an option in cultural studies as a common method employed by anthropologists to inquire about modern society and social matters (Patton, 2005). Ethnography describes culture while understanding lifestyle from the native's view, seen through their artefacts (in this case housing) or behaviour (activities) fundamentally through participant observation and interviews, hence learning from people rather than studying the people (Spradley, 1980). This trait of ethnography fits the concept of comprehending sustainable attributes and features in housing research.

Several housing studies have applied quantitative and qualitative methods separately. However, combining multiple methods of quantitative and qualitative approach enhances research validity because their individual strengths are beneficial and utilised in resolving the weaknesses of each and thus the outcome is optimised. For instance, the mixed method can qualitatively showcase the activity and activity space interaction at the root, sub-urban and urban housing settings. Accordingly results from researcher's observations could triangulate with a questionnaire survey appropriately conducted in order to evaluate the influence of cultural factors of occupants. In the process, explicit findings may evolve through analytically developed categories by searching for patterns and themes (Miles *et al.*, 2013) and also by adopting descriptive and conceptual categorisation strategy (Jennifer, 2002) which forms the basis for theory development (Glaser and Strauss, 1967). Effectively, reflecting core social space uses in housing research that satisfies users' needs and desires as envisaged in sustainable housing design.

Sustainable housing researches require synthesis between socio-cultural determinants uncovered with spatial patterns in creating the direction of influence and establishing core elements of space for design considerations. Thereby, developing design criteria for experts' validation towards ensuring sustainable housing provisions that result in evidence-based design solutions. In the end, sustainable designs emerge from evidence-based design outcome with design indices grounded on explicit indigenous attributes related to a product of the synthesis and convergence of socio-cultural and spatial themes into domains.

Formation of the Research Procedural framework

The evidence from the discussion has posited sustainable housing research in the qualitative realms. However, an in-depth scientific system of inquiry that involves the adoption of several methods and techniques is essential for qualitative research procedure. Amid the steps that constitute the procedure, precise skilful and detailed processes are found as mid-range sub-methods and sub-techniques. These explain specific skills in soliciting data, documentation and analytical procedures worthy of utilisation. Therefore, in facilitating in-depth procedural framework in sustainable housing inquiry researchers could further clarify the procedure using skills that include technique, operational method, operational strategies, operational tactics, detailing instruments and trustworthiness at every stage of the procedure. These steps form a dependable chain-link sequence which analogically pictures the research design while explicitly describing the stages of researcher's engagements and outcomes.

Procedurally, the research goal is achieved effectively when the research operation adopts appropriate techniques. Impliedly techniques in this context refer to the series of steps used to realise the research objectives towards achieving the research operation, while operational methods consist of the process adopted in accomplishing these steps. The concept behind the applied methods form the operational strategies while the operational tactics are mid-range steps that explain the technical skill used within the applied methods. Specifically, outlined tasks across the framework are achieved using instruments as tools. Afterward, the credibility of every sequence of the task is appropriately ensured with skills rooted in the trustworthiness towards a valid outcome that relates the output of every procedural circuit. Significantly, trustworthiness sustains process validity in every qualitative research. A typical procedural chart in a housing research detailing techniques and tactics is illustrated in Table 5.1.

Inhabitants' setting and Population Sampling System

As the urban settings host rural migrants, sustainable urban development can no longer ignore the influence of root and sub-urban space use practices in urban housing design. In this regard, it is worthy to note that typical root settings are traditional, with space arrangement based on culture thus cultural groups could be considered first for ethnographic evaluation. In the process, the activity-space relationship in the layouts of these indigenous groups would be revealed.

Sample sizing in a qualitative study mainly relies on the study's focus, sample frame's reliability and available resources that includes time (Patton, 2002). Despite researchers' efforts in suggesting sample size thresholds for interviews in ethnography, grounded theory, ethnoscience and phenomenology, qualitative studies unlike quantitative studies lacks test for adequacy for sample size approximation (Morse, 1995). Rather it depends on the sample that fits the research question or samples leading to data saturation in the field. Scholars in these situations insist on the consistent sample, bearing in mind sample variations and adopting theoretical and purposive sampling methods.

Table 5.1 Typical Sustainable Housing Research Procedural Chart

Methods	Outcome	Level achieved	Technique	Operational Method	Operational Tactics	Instrument	Trustworthiness
		Establish Research problem	Observation of Phenomenon	Perceived Research problem	Observation	Participant Observer	Engagement with study area
	Establish Research Gap		Previous Knowledge	Extended Observation / Revision of previous knowledge	Focused observation	Participant Observer / Archival documents	Focused Engagement
		Research Objective 1					
	Focused ethnic groups	Identify Major Ethnic Groups & their core dwelling culture attributes	Data Collection	Observation	Focused Observation	Dwellings layouts	Prolonged engagement with study area
	Cultural dwelling attributes		Data analysis	Qualitative factor analysis / Develop domain	Comparison analysis / Theme Analysis	Photographs & Field notes / Coding, theme & domain	
			Data Interpretation	Search for cultural relationship	Review of themes	Cluster of themes	
		Investigate cultural influence in residents spatial transformation					
		Research Objective 2					
		Research Question	Data Collection a. Observation b. Survey	Participant observation / Exploring users' experience / Eliminate weak items / Transformation analysis	Focused Observation / Quantitative methods, Statistical techniques / Observation & Gamma analysis / SEM	Auto-CAD sketches / Survey Questionnaire, SEM / Layout sketches, photographs / narratives, gamma diagrams, SPSS, AMOS	Recorded Field sketches, Instrument validation / Data Triangulation / Method Triangulation / Thresholds & construct validity
			Data Analysis	Psychometric analysis / Result presentation	Search for patterns & / Transformed spaces, Statistical techniques	Tables, figures, photographs, sketches & gamma diagrams, Figures & Tables	Observed analytical process
			Data Interpretation				
		Generate & synthesize cultural determinants & spatial patterns					
	Pattern of influence of core attributes	**Research Objective 3**	Observation	Search for emerging Patterns & elements for design index	Task examination & deduction	Noting themes, patterns & categories	Checking for representativeness, Triangulation, peer/ deferring & expert assessment
		Research Question	Data interpretation	Descriptive discourse / Identification of patterns & influential attributes	Design implication / Revision & description / Synthetic analysis	Categories Matrix	
			Result Presentation			Research question	
	Design Indices	Design attributes grounded on cultural findings					
		Research Objective 4					
		Established Findings	Observation	Converging assertions	Revision	Cultural & Spatial synthesis of themes	
			Observe outcome / Interpret findings				
	Transformation Guide	Culture responsive PH design guide	Research Aim				

Qualitative [subjective] / Quantitative [objective]

Epistemological Knowledge Position

Emancipatory/Naturalistic paradigm

Therefore, in advancing an in-depth examination of the essential phenomenon of sustainable housing research mixed-method sampling strategy is recommended. Because it allows for a study to benefit from the diverse levels involved in the selection process (Teddlie and Yu, 2007). Thus, researchers should aim for data adequacy, by looking out for a progressive data saturation when consistent information no longer produce new themes and patterns to be added to the overall findings. Then, participants and sites could be drawn from a spread of contexts, supported by theoretical sampling technique (Glaser and Strauss, 2009), in order to discover patterns and features of groups. However, since logistics and funding could affect site selections in multi-case study research, samples may be re-directed to show illustrative tendencies of several sites fitness for the research rather than target representativeness. This is in agreement with the view of Robert et al. (2002) on illustrative and representative sample in a case study research.

Additionally, purposeful sampling method allows for the flexibility of both respondents and settings in singles and in groups (Creswell, 2012) and suitable for sustainable housing research due to its subjective nature. As a result, purposeful sampling method is recommended in choosing participants and site in order to reveal the plight of the underestimated and providing data on knowledge about the problem being considered (Creswell, 2012). Advantageously, purposeful sampling technique is credited for its potentials to bring forth reliable results with capabilities of accommodating preference in heterogeneous population (Guarte and Barrios, 2006). Also, it provides a platform to understand effects of social phenomenon in relation to both nature and nurturing human advancement which reveals several research areas. (Patton, 2005). It is noteworthy that purposeful sampling is critiqued for its lack of statistical representativeness of given population, however, it is commendable for qualitative generalization potentials.

Validity and Reliability Tendencies of Sustainable Housing Research

Qualitative research scholars are persistently evaluating and generating validity criteria for qualitative research design, In this regard Maxwell, (1992); Thorne, (1997) and Maxwell, (2012), outlines the criteria at various stages of a qualitative research to include; descriptive validity; interpretive validity; theoretical validity; analytic logic; evaluative validity; generalizable credibility; methodological integrity and interpretive authority. Incessant subjection of qualitative research to the synthesis of validity measures enables decision-making process for researchers and the assessing process for the research audience (Whittemore et al., 2001).

Appropriately, the techniques and procedure embedded in sustainable housing research design and described earlier would ensure suitable credibility and plausibility in the research process. As a result, meaningful and acceptable findings could be achieved. These techniques and procedures cover steps taken to ensure dependability in data, analysis, methods, findings and interpretations.

Research trustworthiness demonstrates the validity and reliability of any study and crucial in qualitative study in order to authenticate the research procedure as well as the accuracy of findings (Le Compte and Goetz, 1982). Equally, Golafshani (2003) refuted and upheld that reliability is not critical in qualitative research as a reliable scale could constantly measure something different from what the researcher intends to measure. Nevertheless, the precision of findings could be achieved from the trio-perspective of the researcher, the participants and the reader (Creswell, 2013; Patton, 1999) relying on the researcher's capability as a participant observer in sourcing rich information to support the analytical process that results in meaningful findings (Patton, 2002). Field situations significantly guide decisions leading to the improved outcome as real site evaluation strategies are compared with standard thresholds. Eventually, the credibility of research outcomes rests substantially with the reader to comprehend the study and adjudge important and suitable outcome (Cutcliffe and McKenna, 1999).

Trustworthiness in Data, Methods and Analysis

The validity of sustainable housing research requires strategies that would ensure trustworthiness at progressive phases. As such, multiple seminal theories and concepts should be used to underpin the foundation to ensure grip and link to knowledge paradigm as well as scientific procedures. Afterwards, Jick (1979) relates that multiple strategies as in this situation bring about consistent and convergent outcomes. In this regard, to ensure transferability of sustainable housing research to related settings phenomenological conditions and details related to participants' choices are necessary. This is consistent with the suggestion of Elo *et al.*, (2014) on ensuring transferability of research to related backgrounds. For instance, participant and site selection based on stratification and randomization improves the research validity through effective representativeness (Miles et al., 2013). Also, adopting several strategies such as focused observation, use of photographs, checklist and assessment of design plans as well as questionnaire survey in seeking data validates research data through data triangulation (Creswell, 2012). Space triangulation strategy could improve the validity of sustainable housing research in seeking data on the same phenomena. Space triangulation implies using diverse settings for both qualitative and quantitative data sourcing and also reaching out to the root, sub-urban and urban settings in order to discover commonalities across space (Berg and Lune, 2004; Denzin, 1989; Kimchi *et al.*, 1991). Therefore, examining space and activity relationships across sampled indigenous communities with such information developed from the field and subjected to member checking straightaway validates the evidence for further analysis. In this situation, the researcher keeps touch with participants in order to re-examine extracts and also ensure their involvement at that stage of field engagement otherwise they might develop less interest later after the entire analytic process of the information sourced (Stake, 2010). Beyond this, triangulation could be used to validate method and results (Erzberger and Kelle, 2003) as triangulation strengthens research (Denzin, 1978). A combined process led result outcome such as the one established in a sustainable housing research from several sources triangulates evidence and increases reliability (Blum and Amy, 2005).

Plausibility of Findings

The credibility of procedural contexts and interpretive process that lead research findings to decisions are enriched by coherent concepts and theories. Miles *et al.* (2013), described numerous strategies for validating findings during interpretation such as noting of patterns and themes; clustering and building of a logical trail of evidence which is suitable for sustainable housing research. Patterns and themes would generate meaning from the outcome of the mixed methods research recommended. In addition, developing categories using clustering approach helps in the appreciating the phenomenon. Whereas developing concepts from attributes of similar kind and patterns towards creating foremost themes describes important claims for assertions. Again Miles *et al.* (2013), recommended strategies for ensuring trustworthiness in deducing conclusions while confirming research findings such as, through searching for representativeness, converging conclusion from triangulation and detecting contrasting evidence. Above all, peer debriefing and expert evaluation of the sustainable housing indices derived from researches further strengthens the validity of the evidence in the research output.

Qualitative Gap: A Subjective Interpretation Space

Concisely, in-depth analytical process of interpreting research findings into claims, theories and assertions are considered subjective both from the positivists' and the constructivists' viewpoint. Thus, qualitative researchers commonly experience "*qualitative jump*" at this stage- a subjective gap that usually occurs when interpretations advance from implicit to explicit themes, domains and categories (Khan, 2008). Assertions and inferences are deduced from findings of analytical processes through this means. The process is a similitude to the operation of the synaptic gap in the human neural system where information is transferred from the axon to the dendrite. During this operation, stimulus generates diverse probable reactions out of which the organs chooses those to give a response. Therefore, several possible valid inferences could emerge from a scientific research process. However, the trail of interpretation relies on the depth of argument by the researcher, the deeper the trial the richer the output but the higher the tendency of the message letting off some meaning. Thus, researchers could get drowned in subjective views hence require imaginative cognition to deduce appropriate research products from interpreting research findings. This is common with housing research where subjective views of both the researcher and the researched characterise the process.

Developing Sustainable Housing Measurable Determinants

In describing sustainable housing parameters, first, there is the need to define the socio-cultural and spatial attributes of housing in the region in order to establish cultural attributes that are connected with the residents. Towards achieving this, attributes are broadly considered under cultural and spatial dimensions in order to create a focus that defines human-space transactions and the operational paradigm of the study. For instance, spatial dimension could include functional households' activity spaces in the building, whereas the socio-cultural dimension may include social principles, lifestyle, identity and households' chores that are exerted on the spatial dimension. Several scholars have aligned with these dimensions, for example, Daramola (2006) advocates that a functional kitchen space should blend with the occupants' lifestyle. Also, Rapoport (1969) acknowledged that house forms are influenced by socio- cultural factors of religion, family structure, privacy, cooking and dining as well as sleeping behaviours. Likewise, courtyards in traditional cultures are considered spaces for women's regular chores (Boyowa, 2005; Muhammad and Said, 2015). In a related study, Kotharkar and Deshpande (2012) listed family structure, occupation, privacy, cooking, eating habits and sacred places as cultural and social determinants of roots' housing configuration. Thus, these provide social meaning of activities that culturally influence house form and are noteworthy in a sustainable housing research particularly in cultured communities. In addition to previous studies, preliminary reconnaissance engagement with the region of study provides acquaintance with housing attributes familiar to the region. However, it is worth acknowledging that each of these functional spaces may likely evoke diverse social meaning to the households.

Conclusion

Remarkably, cultural turn in 21st century sustainable housing research is evident in the appropriate methodological strategy as outlined and advocated by this study. Significantly, culture is a gift bestowed on us as humans and reflecting on our romance with the environment that requires comprehension in defining sustainability in housing research. Remarkably, UN has seen the need to consider socio-cultural issues in attaining sustainable solutions in resolving housing problems. It evaluates inhabitants and their environments by relating their mainstream values as compatible with the natural global viewpoint. So, sustainable housing research could take advantage of seminal underpins from reputable theories such as culture specificity of built environment in Man Environment Relations (Rapoport, 1983); Environment Behaviour Relations (Rapoport, 2000); user centred theory of the built environment (Vischer, 2008); Indegineity (Isah, 2016) as well as cultural paradigm related to the Etic and Emic theory of cross cultural research. Appropriately, ethnographic principles are considered ideal in search for sustainable housing solutions to explicitly describe the socio-cultural influence and user design initiatives towards housing satisfaction. It offers researchers the potential to see housing attributes or features, satisfaction as well as space interaction through the eyes of the end users- the inhabitants of urban settings and ecosystems from a myriad of diverse backgrounds as humans are endowed with cultural diversity. It is, therefore, an effective method for sustainable housing research that reveals users' behaviour as solutions to emergent urban housing challenges.

References

Berg, B. L. and Lune, H. (2004). *Qualitative Research Methods for the Social Sciences*. Pearson: Boston.

Berger, P. L. and Luckmann, T. (1966). The Social Construction of Reality. Garden City, New York: Anchor.

Blum, D. K. and Amy, P. E. (2005). Strategies to win: Six Steps for Creating Problem Statements in Doctoral Research. *Journal of College Teaching and Learning*. 2(11), 47-52.

Boyowa, A. C. (2005). Changing Urban Housing Form and Organization in Nigeria: Lessons for Community Planning. *Planning Perpectives*. 20(1), 69-96.

Creswell, J. W. (2012). *Educational Research Planning, Conducting and Evaluating Quantitative and Qualitative Research*. (4th ed.) Boston, United States of America: Pearson Education Inc.

Creswell, J. W. (2013). *Research design: Qualitative, Quantitative and Mixed Methods Approaches*. London: Sage Publications.

Cutcliffe, J. R. and McKenna, H. P. (1999). Establishing the credibility of Qualitative research findings: the plot thickens. *Journal of Advanced Nursing*. 30(2), 374-380.

Churchil, S. D. (2006). *Phenomenological Analysis: Impression Formation during a Clinical Assessment Interview, in Qualitative Research Methods*, Fischer, C. T. (2006). (ed), Elservier Inc, UK, USA.

Daramola, S. (2006). Affordable and functional housing in a developing economy: A case study of Nigeria. Journal of Land Use and Development Studies. 15(2), 23-28.

Denscombe, M. (2007). *The Good Research Guide for Small-Scale Social Research Projects* (3rd ed.) Portland, Open University Press McGraw-Hill.

Denzin, N. K. (1989). *Interpretive interactionism. Applied social Research Methods series.* Newbury Park: Sage.

Denzin, N. K. and Lincoln, Y. S. (2008). *Strategies of qualitative inquiry.* Thousand Oaks: Sage Publication.

Elo, S., Kääriäinen, M., Kanste, O., Pölkki, T., Utriainen, K. and Kyngäs, H. (2014). *Qualitative Content Analysis A Focus on Trustworthiness.* SAGE Open. 4(1), 2158244014522633.

Eriksson, P. and Kovalainen, A. (2008). *Qualitative methods in Business Research.* Thousand Oaks: Sage Publications.

Erwin, E. J., Brotherson, M. J. and Summers, J. A. (2011). Understanding Qualitative Metasynthesis Issues and Opportunities in Early Childhood Intervention Research. *Journal of Early Intervention.* 33(3), 186-200.

Erzberger, C. and Kelle, U. (2003). Making inferences in mixed methods: The rules of integration. *Handbook of mixed methods in social and behavioural research.* 457-488.

Fellows, R. F. and Liu, A. M. (2009). *Research methods for construction* John Wiley and Sons: US.

Glaser, B. G. and Strauss, A. L. (1967) *The Discovery of Grounded Theory: Strategies for Qualitative Research.* Chicago: Aldine.

Glaser, B. G. and Strauss, A. L. (2009) *The Discovery of Grounded Theory: Strategies for Qualitative Research.* Transaction Publishers.

Golafshani, N. (2003). Understanding Reliability and Validity in Qualitative Research. The Qualitative Report. 8(4), 597-607.

Groat, L. and Wang, D. (2002). *Architectural Research Methods.* Canada: Wiley Publishers.

Guarte, J. M. and Barrios, E. B. (2006). Estimation Under Purposive Sampling. Communication in statistics- *Simulation and Computation,* 35(2), 277-284.

Guba, E. G. and Lincoln, Y. S. (1994). Competing Paradigms in Qualitative Research. *Handbook of Qualitative Research.* 2, 163-194.

Isah A. D. (2015). Culture Integration and Spatial Morphology in Public Housing Transformation in Northern States of Nigeria. Unpublished Ph.D. Thesis, Universiti Teknologi Malaysia.

Isah, A. D. (2016). Urban Public housing in Northern Nigeria: The search for idigeneity and cultural practices in design, Springer International Publishers, Switzerland.

Jennifer, M. (2002). Linking Qualitative and Quantitative Data analysis. In Bryman, A. & Burgess, R.G. (Eds.) *Analysing Qualitative Data.* 29 West 35th Street, New York, NY 10001: Routledge; Taylor & Francis

Jick, T. D. (1979). Mixing Qualitative and Quantitative Methods: Triangulation in action, *Administrative Science Quarterly.* 602-611.

Jonker, J. and Pennink, B. W. (2010). The Essence of Research Methodology, A Concise Guide for Master and PhD Students in Management Science, London, New York, Springer Heidelberg Dordrecht.

Khan T. H. (2008). Living with Transformation: A Study of Self-built Houses in Dhaka, Unpublished PhD Thesis, University of Hong Kong.

Kimchi, J., Polivka, B. and Stevenson, J. S. (1991). Triangulation: Operational definitions. *Nursing Research.* 40(6), 364-366.

Kotharkar, R. and Deshpande, R. (2012). A Comparative Study of Transformations in Traditional House Form: The Case of Nagpur Region, India. Journal of International Society for the study of Vernacular Settlements. 2(2), 17-33.

LeCompte, M. D. and Goetz, J. P. (1982). Problems of reliability and validity in ethnographic research. Review of educational research. 52(1), 31-60.

Lester, S. (1999). An introduction to phenomenological research. Stan Lester Developments. 1-4.

Maxwell, J. A. (1992). Understanding and validity in qualitative research. *Harvard Educational Review.* 62(3), 279-301.

Maxwell, J. A. (2012). *Qualitative Research Design: An Interactive Approach:* Washington DC, Singapore: Sage Publications.

Miles, M. B., Huberman, A. M. and Saldaña, J. (2013). *Qualitative data Analysis: A Methods Sourcebook.* SAGE Publications, Incorporated.

Morgan, D. L. (2007). Paradigms lost and pragmatism regained methodological implications of combining qualitative and quantitative methods. *Journal of Mixed Methods Research.* 1(1), 48-76.

Morris, E. W. and Winter, M. (1975). A theory of Family Housing Adjustment. *Journal of Marriage and the Family.* 79-88.

Morse, I. J. M. (1995) *Completing a qualitative project: Details and dialogue,* Thousand Oaks, CA: Sage.

Muhammad, I. B., & Said, I. (2015). Behavioural use of courtyard in a Nupe cultural landscape of Nigeria *Interdisciplinary Behaviour and Social Sciences* 227-232: CRC Press.

Oliver, M. (1992). Changing the social relations of research production? Disability, *Handicap & Society.* 7(2), 101-114.

Oliver, M. (1997). Emancipatory research: realistic goal or impossible dream. *Doing Disability Research.* 2, 15-31.

Patton, M. Q. (1999). Enhancing the quality and credibility of qualitative analysis. *Health Services Research.* 34(5 Pt 2), 1189.

Patton, M. Q. (2002). *Qualitative Research and Evaluation Methods.* (3rd ed.) Thousand Oaks, California 91320: Sage Publications, Inc.

Patton, M. Q. (2005). *Qualitative Research.* Wiley Online Library.

Rapoport, A. (1969). *House Form and Culture.* Englewood Cliffs: Prentice-hall.

Rapoport, A. (1983). Development, culture change and supportive design. *Habitat International.* 7(5), 249-268.

Rapoport, A. (2002). Theory, culture and housing. Housing, theory and society (Incomplete). 17(4), 145-165.

Robert, G. B., Christopher, J. P., Keith, E. and Christine, P. (2002). Four studies from one or one study from four? Multi-site case study research. In Alan, B. & Robert, G. B. (Eds.) *Analysisng Qualitative Data.* 29 West 35th Street, New York, NY 10001: Routledge; Taylor & Francis

Stake, R. E. (2010). *Qualitative Research: Studying how things work.* New York, London: Guilford Press.

Starks, H. and Trinidad, S. B. (2007). Choose your method: A comparison of Phenomenology, Discourse analysis, and Grounded theory. *Qualitative Health Research.* 17(10), 1372-1380.

Spradley, J. P. (1980). *Participant Observation,* United States: Holt, Rinehart and Winston.

Teddlie, C. (2005). Methodological Issues Related to Causal Studies of Leadership A Mixed Methods Perspective from the USA. *Educational Management Administration & Leadership.* 33(2), 211-227.

Teddlie, C. and Yu, F. (2007). Mixed Methods Sampling A Typology With Examples. *Journal of Mixed Methods Research.* 1(1), 77-100.

Thorne, S. (1997). The art (and science) of critiquing qualitative research. In Morse, I. J. M. (Ed.) *Completing a Qualitative Project: Details and Dialogue* (pp. 117-132). Thousand Oaks, CA: Sage.

Vischer, J. C. (2008). Towards a user-centred theory of the built environment. *Building Research & Information.* 36(3), 231-240.

Walsh, D. and Downe, S. (2005). Meta-synthesis method for qualitative research: A literature review. *Journal of Advanced Nursing.* 50(2), 204-211.

Whittemore, R., Chase, S. K. and Mandle, C. L. (2001). Validity in qualitative research. *Qualitative Health Research.* 11(4), 522-537.

Willig, C. (2001). *Introducing Qualitative Research in Psychology Adventures in Theory and Method.* Buckingham, 325 Chestnut Street Philadelphia, PA 19106, USA: Open University Press.

Woodside, A. G. (2010). *Case Study Research: Theory, Methods and Practice: Theory, Methods, Practice.* United Kingdom: Emerald Group Publishing.

Yin, R. K. (2014). *Case study research: Design and methods.* Thousand Oaks, California Sage publications.

Chapter 6

Ethnography as a sustainable approach to cultural landscape studies: A case of Nupe community in central Nigeria

Isa Bala Muhammad

Department of Architecture,
Federal University of Technology, Minna, Nigeria

mib@futminna.edu.ng

Abstract: Cultural landscapes are referred to as the way people relate to their environment and the meaning as well as the values they derive from such transactions. Understanding cultural landscape transactions through the perspective of the native people requires a social science research method that captures people's cultural values about their landscape. One of such methodological approach is ethnography. Ethnography is associated with the immersion of the researcher in the field, and it draws on a family of methods which includes participant observations, listening, and interviews. These multiple methods of data collection that are subsumed in ethnography are complex, most especially when it is used in cultural landscape research. As such this study gives a detailed outline of how ethnography was employed in the study of a cultural landscape of Nupe ethnic group in central Nigeria. The chapter gives a written account of the experiences of the researcher which also had to take cognisance of the role of theory and philosophical paradigm in social science research. Furthermore, the chapter gives an account of the procedure followed in establishing the philosophical paradigm as well as how the reliability and validity of data elicited were ensured. Most importantly is the applicability of the ethnographic process in the study of other cultural landscapes.

Key words: Cultural landscape, Ethnography, Heritage, Cultural values, Sustainability

Introduction

The preservation of cultural landscape resources is necessary because its study is relevant in a lot of sectors such as rural development, nature conservation, and forestry. Cultural landscape study is also an essential element in the interpretation of sustainable development (Agnoletti, 2006). More recently, the United Nations General Assembly report also established and recognised the preservation of cultural and natural heritage, including biodiversity and landscapes

(United-Nations, 2016), The dynamics of the cultural landscape have been seen to trigger socio-economic development where the relationship between man and the environment has over a long period of time created cultural values (Tengberg et al., 2012; Türkyılmaz, 2016). However, the herculean task is the choice of an appropriate method in the study as well as an understanding of these values within the frame of the people who inhabit such landscapes. This is even more profound when cultural landscape values are to be interpreted to include both tangible and intangible values (del Barrio, Devesa, & Herrero, 2012; WHC, 1994). This arises from the confusion faced by a researcher who chooses ethnography as a technique for social enquiry (Mannay & Morgan, 2014). In response, this chapter focuses on creating a step by step process followed in the use of ethnography for the study of a cultural landscape.

The first part of this chapter focuses on the philosophical paradigm and the theoretical framework applied to the elicitation of information on cultural landscape values. As such the two main philosophical paradigms, Positivism and constructivism were discussed and how each of the paradigms is situated in the study. Furthermore, the grounded theory is also discussed as a frame that guided the explorative research as well as its appropriateness towards analysis of the data elicited through participant observation. In the researcher's eight-month data collection process, the study focused on the everyday lives of the indigenous people residing within the studied Nupe community.

Also, in this chapter I offer a reflection on the research, the documented immersion in the field towards the understanding of the meaning of landscape and values people associate with their landscape. As such, the analytical process towards the formulation of grounded theory as well as the processes through which the cultural landscape values' variables were determined is discussed. The chapter concludes with the steps taken towards ensuring reliability and validity of the methods used for data collection and analysis.

Situating Philosophical Paradigm for Cultural Landscape Studies

A philosophical paradigm is a theoretical framework and system employed to view events (Fellows & Liu, 2008). It elaborates and shows views and perspectives that are adopted in the determination of a phenomenon. Cultural landscape transactions are based on peoples' cultural activities (Berker, 2011) and one of the most suitable means of gathering the total experience and perception of people, is through an unstructured exploration (Blommaert & Jie, 2010). It is also to be noted that for a sociological phenomenon, a qualitative form of data also helps in the understanding of people's world view (Glaser & Strauss, 2009). More also is that human, unlike other objects of study are complex; they hold certain values and live in the world which has meaning and have actions that are intelligible and therefore only understood through empirical evidence

(Miles, Huberman, & Saldaña, 2013). In the elicitation of empirical evidence about people-place relationship, there exists a clear distinction in the philosophical school of thought between positivism and constructivism. Each of the paradigms has its weaknesses and strengths. The strength of each method depends on the type of study and data that is to be elicited. As a result of this, the next section explains what guided the choice of philosophical paradigm for the study of cultural landscape of the Nupe community.

Positivism and Cultural Landscape Study

The positivists are inclined towards Cartesian duality of the existence of reality which stipulates that there are observable facts out there in the field that can be measured by an observer (Creswell, 2012). This thus showcases the positivists to be inclined towards quantitative data which makes the researcher completely detached from the investigation (Biklen, 2010). The positivists believe that social observations should be treated like the way physical scientist treat physical phenomena (Goldkuhl & Cronholm, 2010). However, to understand the cultural landscape values of a community, it is nearly impossible to affirm an absolute true situation, because culture differs and so do the landscapes (Gullino & Larcher, 2012). Suggesting that, there exists a little chance for the existence of the universal reality in cultural landscape transactions (Rapoport, 1969). Consequent upon this, the philosophical paradigm of positivism is unsuitable for the study of cultural landscape values. This is because the cultural landscape is inclined toward people's perception and cultural values which are not all tangibly represented. Suggesting that for a cultural landscape study, absolute reality does not exist in what people perceive and value.

Constructivism and Cultural Landscape Study

The constructivist paradigm posits that construct realities are bound and that, time and context are free from generalisation (Miles et al., 2013). It also advocates that truth and reality are attained through the perspectives of the participants. Similarly, cultural landscape transaction is associated with observations of phenomena which involve the understanding of where, when and how, transactions are conducted (Stephenson, 2010). It also requires the understanding of the sense in which such transactions are perceived by the people (Bergeron, Paquette, & Poullaouec-Gonidec, 2014). It is to be noted that the type of landscape and the culture of people affect how transactions of people are carried out. Thus, the uniqueness of each landscape and its culture means that there exists no absolute reality as far as the human relationship with the environment is concerned. It, therefore, becomes more plausible to be inclined to the constructivist philosophical paradigm in the study of cultural landscape values of communities.

However, the complexity associated with cultural landscapes' research has to contend with culture and human behaviour. Furthermore, the perception of people about their landscape requires a long stay with careful observations (Stephenson, 2010). As such, for phenomenological research on the cultural landscape values, ethnography becomes a suitable means for elicitation of information (O'Reilly, 2009).

The Study Community

Rural landscapes are largely historic products that need to be protected from rapid urbanisation (Agnoletti, 2014). More also is that opportunities are bound in Africa towards its contribution to humankind in the world of science, technology and culture. This is because Africa is considered as the cradle of humanity (United-Nations, 2002). This cradle of humanity, (Africa) is made up of several ethnic groups each with its uniqueness and cultural landscape transactions which have limited documentation especially the minority ethnic groups. For example, Nigeria has over 250 ethnic groups and one of such ethnic group is the Nupe which has been affirmed to have a rich cultural heritage (Nadel, 1937, 1942). As such this methodology (ethnography) was used to measure people and space interaction in a rural Nupe community of Doko, Nigeria. The choice of Doko community is based on its historical connection as one of the communities that constituted the nucleus of Nupe kingdom (Muhammad & Said, 2015). It is located 12 kilometres south-west of Bida in Niger State, Nigeria. The landscape of the community is surrounded by a hill that runs from the south down to the west as indicated in Figure 6.1.

Doko Hill

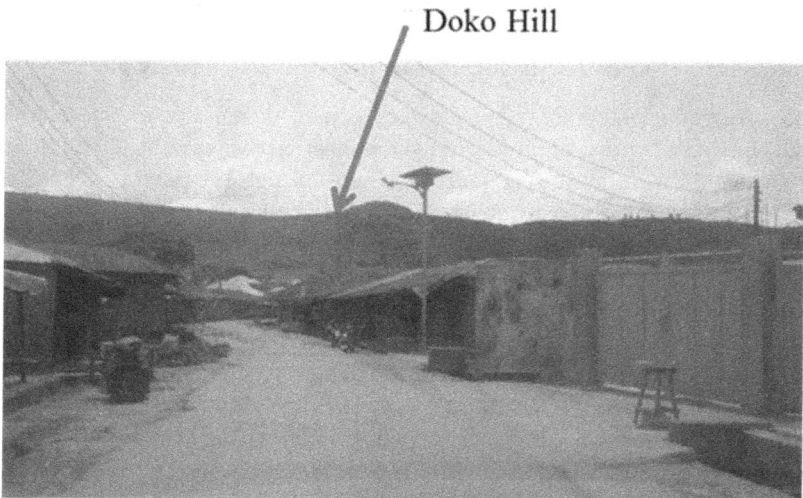

Figure 6.1 The hill surrounding Doko Community landscape

Soliciting Information through Ethnography

Ethnography is engendered in an in-depth study, which involves the interpretation of meaning in the local context of the participants. As such it is rooted in the first-hand exploration of research settings (Mannay & Morgan, 2014). Ethnography when used for the collection of data , requires the researcher to be immersed in the field to collect information about the study phenomena (Murchison, 2010). The ethnographer, therefore, collects data by interacting with respondents which usually take different forms such as conversations, interviews, and performance of ritual within the community. Ethnography allows emphasis to be placed more on understanding the meaning and the cultural practice of the people within the settings where they inhabit.

The ethnographic mode of eliciting information from the Nupe Community was saddled with the challenges of conducting it in either covert or overt form. This challenge of overt observation was based on the influence of the observer on what is being studied (Patton, 2005). Because there exists the possibility of the behaviour of those being studied to be staged with the resultant effect of affecting the data elicited (Oliver and Eales, 2008). On the other hand, covert observations would have resulted in ethical questions. This is because, it is also argued that, it is the right of those being studied to know that they are being studied (O'Reilly, 2009). This conflict cuts across all the facet of ethnographic field work right from the type of observation, evaluator's role to participants, and the portrayal of the purpose of the evaluation to the people being studied (Risjord, 2007). Consequently, the strategy employed in the field was to adopt a process that was most suitable, reliable and ethically viable. As such for the study of the cultural landscape of the studied community, the emphasis was laid on the fulfilment of ethical issues as well as ensuring that the data gathered were valid (Miles et al., 2013). Patton (1987), gave five dimensions through which empirical field work varies. They are the role of the evaluator, the portrayal of the evaluator role to others, the portrayal of the purpose of the evaluation to others, duration of the evaluation and the focus of the evaluation. In a similar manner, the dimension that was taken for the study of cultural landscape of the Nupe community is given in Figure 6.2.

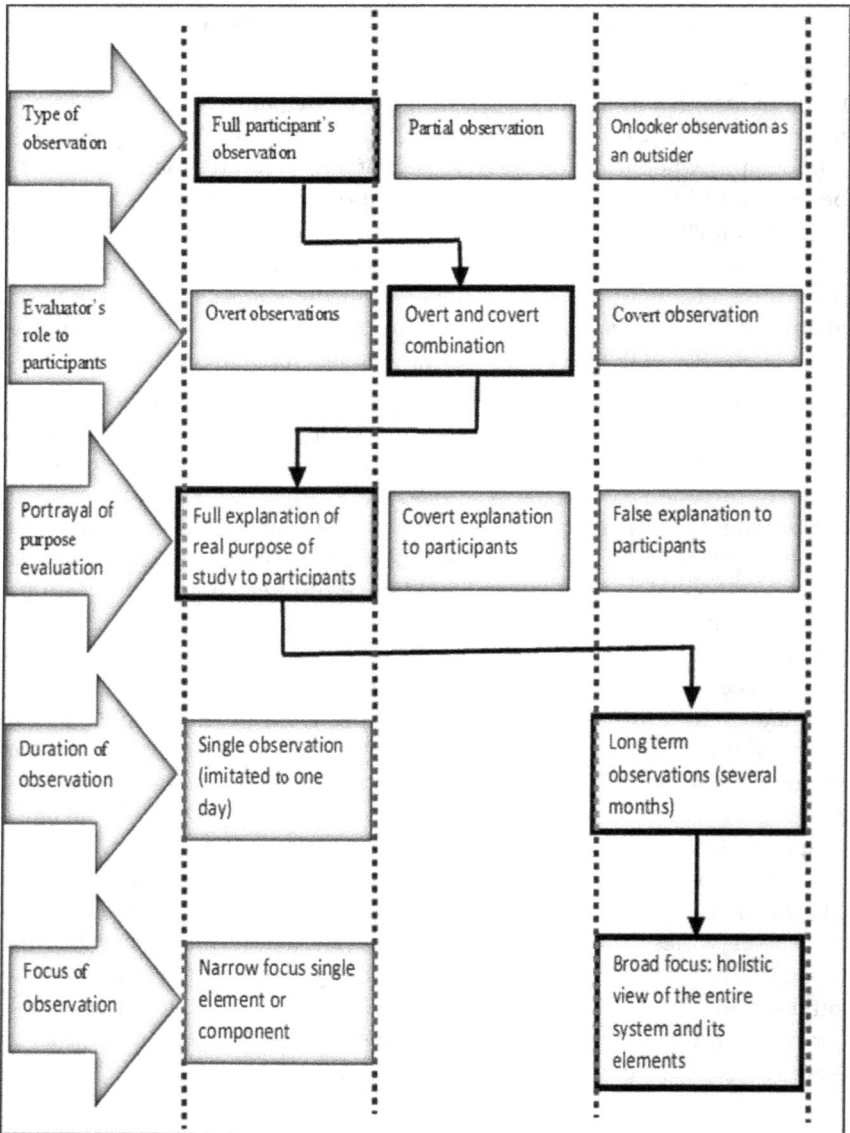

Figure 6.2 Dimension for the conduct of the fieldwork on the Nupe cultural landscape, adopted from (Patton, 1987)

The elicitation of data from the community required a choice between three types of observations which are either full participant's observation, partial observation or an onlooker observation. Markedly, rural communities are characterised by the settings in which everyone is known due to their small population. As such the conduct of research which is ethnographic and which also involves a long time of stay makes it nearly impossible not to be noticed. It thus necessitated that the choice of type of observation needed to be a full observation. Therefore, the Village Head was informed of the study as well as its purpose. The approval of the Community Head allowed for some level of trust and rapport to be developed between the researcher and the community. Trust, especially in ethnographic research, is key for the gathering of information from participants (Charmaz, 2014).

Period of Stay for Holistic Understanding of Cultural Landscape

In anthropological tradition, participant observation requires a minimum of six months to be spent in the culture of those being observed (Patton, 2005). This is because the holistic view of people's culture takes a great deal of time and the social scientific objective is to generate theoretical propositions of how a culture functions. As such the duration for the elicitation of data on the cultural landscape took 8 months. This is to allow for most of the transaction of the community to be captured. This included farming activities such as the planting and harvest periods in the community. More also is that the long stay allowed for transactions of the community to be observed over the period of wet and dry seasons. The reason for this is that climatic condition most times have an influence on how people interact with their spaces. Additionally, in rural communities, especially in Nigeria, the activities of the wet seasons mostly do take place at the farm while that of the dry season are off the farm (Muhammad, 2017). Furthermore, in order to have a full understanding of the community transactions, aside from participant observation, interviews were conducted as part of the ethnographic process.

Determination of Geographic Boundaries in Cultural Landscapes

The scale of data to be elicited in cultural landscape study is an important factor that needs to be established right from the beginning. As such, the scale of observations for the studied community was established to be the domestic space as well as the geographic extent required by the natives towards the fulfilment of their daily needs (Appleton, 1975). The socio-cultural transaction of each community is established based on the family system and as such the determination of the family basic transactions gives the cue to the spatial transactions of the community. Thus, the ethnography study began with the understanding of the homestead, which is the domestic space.

Observation of the Domestic Space Transactions

Domestic spatial relationships are central to cultural landscape transaction more also is that it constitutes a great proportion of an individual's daily life (Ausserhofer et al., 2016). As such it became imperative to understand the socio-physical settings of the Nupe domestic space (Alitajer & Molavi Nojoumi, 2016). Therefore, the determination of domestic space transactions of the community, a detailed sketch of some selected compounds was made. It involved the identification of tangible features that constitute each compound. This was necessary so as to determine the conceptualization of the traditional architecture of the Nupe people. More also is that it is expected just like many cultures, that the Nupes will have a unique characterisation of their vernacular architecture (Donovan & Gkartzios, 2014). Undoubtedly, the community's compound layout showcased a common character after 15 compounds were documented. The features found common in all the compounds visited are the *kata* (bedrooms), the *katagi* (kitchen), *nanche* (open kitchen) *katamba* (entrance hut), *zhempa* (courtyard), *yekun* (the local oven structure), *edo* (granary), *Kara* (fence), *shikpata* (toilets and bathrooms) and *ega* (animal pen). Some of these features observed are shown in Figure 6.3, 6.4 and 6.5 respectively.

Figure 6.3 A typical Nupe compound showing the kata (bedroom), katagi (kitchen) Nanche (open kitchen) and zhempa (courtyard)

Figure 6.4 The katamba (entrance hut) found in most of the compounds

Figure 6.5 *Ega* (Animal pen) in different forms in most compounds

The people-place relationship is complex to measure due to the dynamics associated with what people do every day, especially in domestic spaces. The technique found most useful for the everyday behaviour of the built environment is the time budget concept (Muhammad & Said, 2015). Time budget concept entails the collection of what people do during a fixed period of time. Such type of observations is carried out either through diaries or through the conduct of interviews with the participant. However, for the cultural landscape transactions of the studied community, the administration of diaries to the participants was not possible due to the low level of literacy and thus asking the participants to document their activities was difficult. As a result, the researcher decided to map the activities of family members in a chart. This involved the monitoring of activities base on sessions. Session 1 was held between 6 am and 3 pm, session 2 was held between 3 pm and 9 pm, and finally, the 3rd session lasted from 9 pm to 6 am. These seasons were based on preliminary observations made on the pattern of the community's transactions. A day was then set aside each for the selected families (n=15). Sessions 1 and 2 were logged in through direct observation while the 3rd session, which constituted the private time for night rest were mostly captured the following day through interviews. The interviews were conducted on the *emitso* (family heads) and *inna-emitso* (women's head). These interviews were made to capture the activities that took place during the private time of the Night. As such the inclusion of the interviews together with observations allowed for a 24-hour circle of activities of each of the families observed.

Furthermore, a follow-up random visits were made to the compounds to intersect the bias associated with human subjects, especially when they are aware that they are being observed (Patton, 2005). This strategy was taken to also ensure that each session was covered at least thrice in each of the 15 compounds chosen for the study. This was to validate the participant's observations (Blommaert & Jie, 2010). It was equally important that during the process of data collection photographs were taken. Photographs aside from its presentations of empirical truth, they were referred to later in order to give a clearer understanding of the activity log. Besides, photographs do offer experiences in which linguistic terms cannot completely interpret or explain (Seamon, 2014).

Similarly, during the conduct of observations, in the spatial transaction of families, there existed periods in which the activities were broken. Such periods included long hours of rainfall during the day and night. This natural phenomenon forced activities that usually take place outside to be suspended and refuge sought in covered spaces such as rooms, entrance huts, and kitchens. These periods of activity transactions were excluded because they did not constitute the normal routine of the families. Obviously, it is expected that people-place daily transactions are likely to be broken by occasional external forces (Seamon, 2015). As such in the study of people-place relationship what needs to be understood are the routine transactions that occur without any external interference. Summarily, the observation within the domestic space was directed by a set of ethnographic observation guide as illustrated in Table 6.1.

Table 6.1 Observation guide on the Domestic space transactions

1	How are the buildings and compounds laid out?
2	What are the physical features that constitute a typical compound?
3	What are the distances between major activities within the compound?
4	What are the meeting places?
5	How are the compounds kept clean?
6	What is the source of water?
7	How do they source for their cooking fuel?
8	Where do the female family members spend most of their time?
9	Where do the male family members spend most of their time?
10	Which part of the compound do children spend most of their time?
11	Where do most men receive their guests?
12	Where do most females receive their guests?
13	Where do men eat their food?
14	Where do women eat their food?
15	Where do the family members have their meetings?
16	How are spaces defined for males and females within the family?
17	How is security constituted within the compound?

The outline of domestic space transactions, schedule as shown in Table 6.1 is to ensure that, the data elicited across the various families observed are the same. This was done so that ng a pattern could be established as the cultural, spatial transactions of Nupe families within their domestic spaces.

Observations of the Community's Transactions

Cultural landscape study deals with various forms of transactions. It, therefore requires that data elicitation is carried out systematically to save time and also to ensure that relevant data about the phenomenon is captured (O'Reilly, 2009). Although the study on the cultural landscape of the Nupe community was explorative, it was important that the research was carried out within a given frame of reference (Forsey, 2010). Correspondingly, the "Habitat Theory" was used as a frame of reference for the study due to its universal applicability in the study of cultural landscapes. The habitat theory asserts that people interact with their environment towards the attainment of their biological needs. It further posits that settlements exist only in a landscape that provides

water, food, security, defence and place for economic activities. Correspondingly the researcher ensured that aside from other findings that emerged,
observations were also made to see how defence, security, water, food, and
shelter were constituted within the studied community.

Furthermore, the plethora of data collected required categorisation for
ease and also accurate elicitation of information (Creswell, 2012). Consequently, Nassauer's (1995) three distinctive classification of cultural landscape was employed. They are "Form", "Practice" and "Relationship". The
data elicited under "Form" are the spatial and physical structure of both
natural and man-made, while data on "Practice" is the transactions of the
people between themselves and the landscape while "Relationship" includes those transactions that are intangible. The sum of these classes of
data is represented in Figure 6.6.

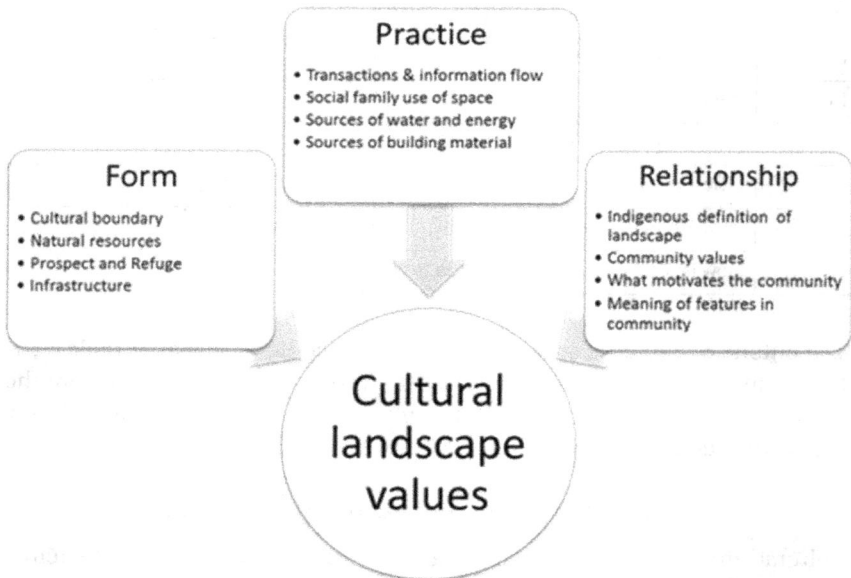

Figure 6.6 The three Key variables of cultural landscape values

It is to be noted that the constituents of the "relationship" category are
mainly made up of meanings and values of the community. As such this
category is difficult to measure through observations. It thus became necessary to use interviews as a suitable tool for understanding the intangible
values of the Nupe community.

The Interview Approach for determination of Intangible Values

One of the important sources of information on participant observation is the interview (Forsey, 2010). The interview serves as a means for learning about things that cannot directly be observed such as feeling, thoughts and what goes on in the natural world of those being studied. However, three types of interview approaches are available for the elicitation of information. They are the general interview guide approach, the conversational interview, the standardised open-ended interview. The general interview guide approach consists of questions carefully worded which mean that each respondent is taken through the same sequence of questions (Creswell, 2012). Its limitation lies in its confinement to an outline of predetermined questions which will result in information being gathered under limited subjects. Moreover, phenomenological studies require information to be gathered naturally from the participants (Seamon, 2015). As such the use of conversational interview became more suitable especially during the early part of the field work when the rapport between the researcher and the community was being established. More also is that the choice of conversational interview allowed for flexibility on questions asked by the researcher towards the understanding of the community's culture and values. Similarly, conversations with participants afforded the researcher an in-depth understanding as well as the subjective meaning the participants ascribe to their landscape (Mannay & Morgan, 2014).

In addition, the adoption of conversational interview suited all categories of respondents, which included children, and the adults (Forsey, 2010). The advantage of this is that the researcher was able to interview the indigenous people through their own terminologies, perceptions, and experiences. Furthermore, the data elicited was such that it was gathered in the natural state of the people and as such, it reduced the complexities in the understanding of people's socio-cultural transactions. Buttressing this is Shopes (2011) in which she stated that good information from the field means the ability for the respondent to give freely the necessary information without the feeling of holding back some information. It is important that in the conduct of interviews in cultural landscapes, key informants need to be identified in order to get adequate information about their community. In the case of Nupe community, the compounds heads are the custodians of the cultural heritage of the community. Therefore, the compound heads became the key informants in each of the compounds visited. The interviews were all in the evenings after their day's work at the farm. It is important that appropriate time is strategically used so as to get adequate information from the respondents.

It is worth mentioning that aside from the compound heads, interviews were also conducted on the women, children, and people whose transactions were seen to be different from the general practice of the community which is mainly farming. The examples of these categories are the *gozan* (traditional barber), and the *egba* (the local builder). This was to ensure that most of the transactions of the community were adequately captured. In addition, an audio recorder was used to record interview responses, The choice of an audio recorder over a video recorder was because it was less intrusive and allows the respondents to adjust quickly as the interview progressed (Mehl, Gosling, & Pennebaker, 2006).

Ethnographic Data Analysis

Ethnographic experience in the cultural landscape of community is the culmination of diverse sources of data which included participant's observations, taking of photographs, interviews and field notes. Field notes were taken in the form of sketches and jottings of the researcher on what was observed (O'Reilly, 2009). However, the first aspect of the data analysis for all the various forms of qualitative information was to employ open coding, then followed by sorting (Miles et al., 2013). Employing this sequence of analysis of open coding and sorting was carried out towards answering of questions such as when, where, why, who and how transactions are made (Charmaz, 2014).

As such for this study, the whole data collected were defragmented into a pool. Even though, as earlier mentioned information about the cultural landscape transactions of the Nupe community was collected under three categories of "Form", "Practice" and "Relationship". However, these categories were used as a framework for the elicitation of data and thus the grouping did not emerge from analysis of cultural landscape data. Therefore, there was the need for the generation of an indigenous typology based on the settings under study (Miles *et al.*, 2013). As such, to generate an indigenous typology, all information gathered under the three categories was merged as illustrated in Figure 6.7 for content analysis. Thereafter, computer software QSR Nvivo 10 was used because of its capabilities in content analysis and organisation of documents, such as audio, video, pictures, and memos.

The information from pictures, field notes, sketches, and interviews was aggregated together to create codes. These codes were then thematically analysed and label given to describe each category of the theme (Figueroa, 2008). The thematic analysis output emerged with five categories of themes which are "Profession", "Architecture", "Family structure", "Landscape" and "Values" as illustrated in Figure 6.8.

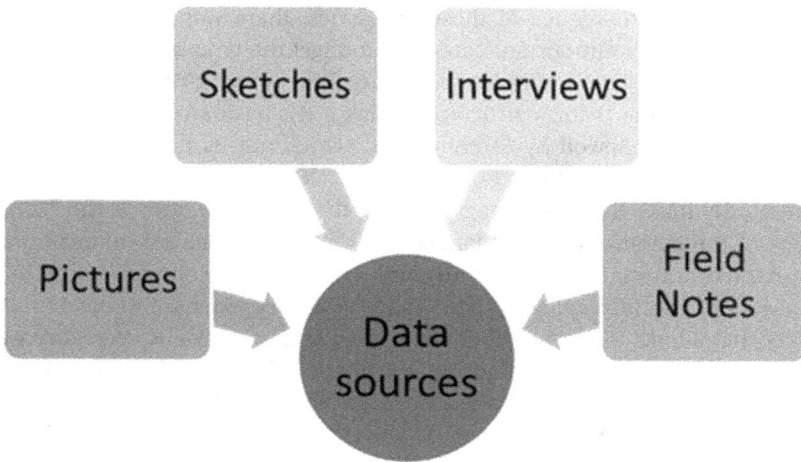

Figure 6.7 Multiple sources of ethnographic data (Muhammad 2015)

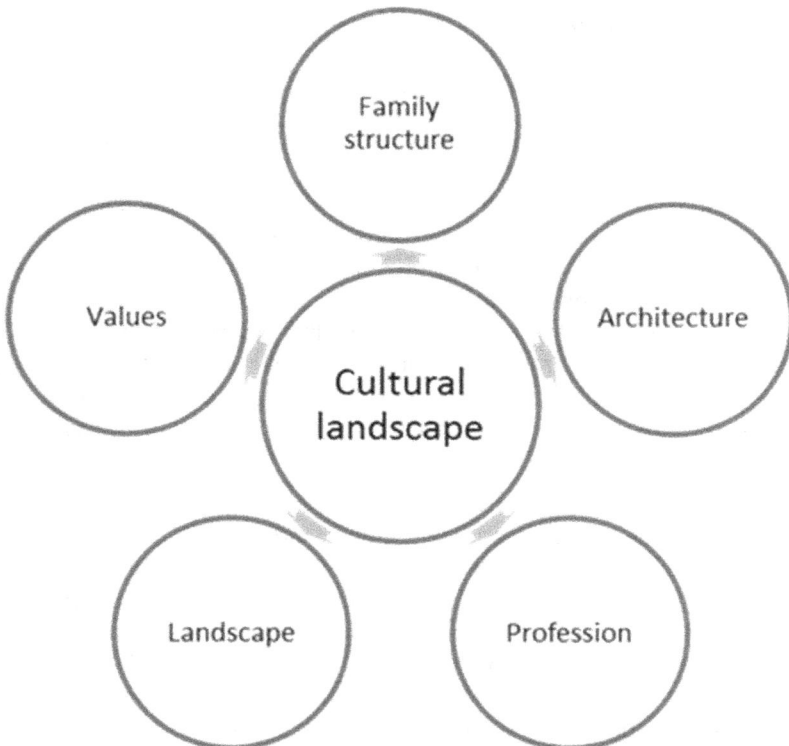

Figure 6.8 The Emergent Five Categories of Themes for Nupe Community Cultural Landscape (Muhammad 2015)

Thereupon the emergence of these categories, there was also the need to determine the most important category amongst the typologies of categories towards the formulation of grounded theory (Miles *et al.*, 2013). To restate, the first category is the "Family structure" which is the basic structure of communities; this was followed by "Architecture" which means the immediate domestic space of both built and unbuilt forms. "People and profession" of the community make the third category, while the fourth category is the "Landscape of the community". The landscape was operationalized to mean both the natural and man-made features and spaces of the common communal transaction. The fifth category, the "Value" category emerged to have multidimensional links to all the other categories. Thus, the "Value" category was found suitable for the generation of a grounded theory of the community (Charmaz, Clarke, Friese, & Washburn, 2015; Glaser, Strauss, & Strutzel, 1968). The foregoing analysis showcased an inductive grounding of data and also abstractions from the cultural landscape of the community. More also is that the strength of ethnography lies in allowing the unexpected and also an unpredictable outcome of research. This thus makes it devoid of techniques that insist on control of outcomes (Mannay & Morgan, 2014).

Reliability and Validity of Ethnographic Data

Reliability and Validity of data for ethnographic data (qualitative data) are difficult especially when it has to do with the establishment of a uniform standard of measurement to be applied everywhere (Seamon & Sowers, 2008). However, reliability can be obtained through intersubjective corroboration. As such for this study, the researcher within the limits of knowledge imbibed the principles of reporting the phenomenon with vividness, such that the reader is drawn to the text in the form of reality and honesty (Forsey, 2010). Accuracy was attained through maximisation of believability of the reader and also a comparison with other similar or contrasting scenarios. The ultimate aim was towards drawing the reader from their usual recognition towards a new path of understanding (Seamon, 2009).

Furthermore, the reliability of the data was certified by the use of multiple methods in data gathering on the cultural landscape values of the study community. To rephrase, this included interviews and participants observations. Direct participation provided a meaningful context of what took place and what people actually did empirically and therefore gave the data more credence. More also is that participants observation followed by interview reinforced the quality of data gathered (Miles *et al.*, 2013). In addition, reporting on rival explanations lends credibility to the final sets of findings reported by the evaluator. Hence, negative cases were sought within the community and in some instances corroborations or counters, found during the course of the discussion. Similarly, extrapolations were also made to give a multiple interest and possibilities of the same scenario within the studied community and also on other studies carried out elsewhere. Doing this was to allow the researcher a broad-based view of all phenomena studied. Finally, the sequence of a good phenomenological study as outlined by Seamon and Sowers (2008) was followed. This involved the identifications of phenomena, descriptive account of the phenomena, and the study of the respondent towards understanding the underlying commonalities and pattern.

Additionally, the generation of grounded theory is towards the fulfilment of four criteria which are fit, work, relevance and modifiability (Creswell, 2012). As such, for fitness, it was ensured that there were no contradictions of what were uttered, especially in the interviews and the realities on the ground. While in workability of data, it was ensured that variations found in the field were explained. Such explanations were also made within the context of the cultural landscape values of the studied community. Finally, the theory formulated was made amendable to new information. Consequent upon these all the four criteria of grounded theory were fulfilled.

Conclusion

Sustainable development, advocates for the incorporation of people's values in developments. However, people's values are constituted in both tangible and intangible forms. It thus becomes imperative to have a systematic way of understanding such values. People's values are constituted in their cultural landscapes which serve as an everyday environment. The study showcased the extensive step by step process involved in the elicitation of cultural landscape values of communities. These, amongst others, included the formation of rapport with the study community, the use of multi-method approach in the elicitation of data about the indigenous people upon which the bedrock of the information was ethnographic. The ethnographic process allowed for data to be gathered and understood through the perspective of the indigenous people. Most importantly is that rural landscapes are largely historic products that need to be understood and protected from global acculturation towards documentation and preservation of the uniqueness of each cultural landscape. Consequently, ethnography as a methodological approach needs to be sustained as a sustainable means in the study of cultural landscapes in order to meet up with United Nations advocacy in the preservation of global cultural heritages.

References

Agnoletti, M. (2006). *The conservation of cultural landscapes:* Oxfordshire, United Kingdom: CAB Internation.

Agnoletti, M. (2014). Rural landscape, nature conservation and culture: Some notes on research trends and management approaches from a (southern) European perspective. *Landscape and urban planning 126*, 66-73. doi: http://dx.doi.org/10.1016/j.landurbplan.2014.02.012

Alitajer, S., & Molavi Nojoumi, G. (2016). Privacy at home: Analysis of behavioural patterns in the spatial configuration of traditional and modern houses in the city of Hamedan based on the notion of space syntax. *Frontiers of Architectural Research, 5*(3), 341-352. doi: http://dx.doi.org/10.1016/j.foar.2016.02.003

Appleton, J. (1975). *The experience of landscape.* Great Britain: John Wiley and Sons, Ltd.

Ausserhofer, D., Deschodt, M., De Geest, S., van Achterberg, T., Meyer, G., Verbeek, H., ... Engberg, S. (2016). "There's No Place Like Home": A Scoping Review on the Impact of Homelike Residential Care Models on Resident-, Family-, and Staff-Related Outcomes. *Journal of the American Medical Directors Association, 17*(8), 685-693. doi: http://dx.doi.org/10.1016/j.jamda.2016.03.009

Bergeron, J., Paquette, S., & Poullaouec-Gonidec, P. (2014). Uncovering landscape values and micro-geographies of meanings with the go-along method. *Landscape and urban planning, 122*, 108-121.

Berker, T. (2011). Domesticating Spaces Sociotechnical Studies and the Built Environment. *Space and Culture, 14*(3), 259-268.

Biklen, S. (2010). The Quality of evidence in Qualitative research. *International Encyclopedia of Education,* 488-497.

Blommaert, J., & Jie, D. (2010). *Ethnographic fieldwork: A beginner's guide:* Channel View Books: UK.

Charmaz, K. (2014). *Constructing grounded theory.* London: Sage.

Charmaz, K. C., Clarke, A. E., Friese, C., & Washburn, R. (2015). *Situational analysis in practice: Mapping research with grounded theory.* London: Left Coast Press.

Creswell, J. W. (2012). *Educational Research Planning, Conducting and Evaluating Quantitative and Qualitative Research* (P. A. Smith Ed. 4th ed.). Boston: Pearson Education Inc.

Del Barrio, M. J., Devesa, M., & Herrero, L. C. (2012). Evaluating intangible cultural heritage: The case of cultural festivals. *City, Culture and Society, 3*(4), 235-244. doi: http://dx.doi.org/10.1016/j.ccs.2012.09.002

Donovan, K., & Gkartzios, M. (2014). Architecture and Rural Planning:'Claiming the Vernacular'. *Land Use Policy, 41*, 334-343.

Fellows, R. F., & Liu, A. M. (2008). *Research methods for construction.* United Kingdom: Wiley-Blackwell.

Figueroa, S. K. (2008). The Grounded Theory and the Analysis of Audio-Visual Texts. *International Journal of Social Research Methodology, 11*(1), 1-12. doi: 10.1080/13645570701605897

Forsey, M. G. (2010). Ethnography as participant listening. *Ethnography, 11*(4), 558-572.

Glaser, B. G., & Strauss, A. L. (2009). *The discovery of grounded theory: Strategies for qualitative research:* Transaction Publishers : London, UK.

Glaser, B. G., Strauss, A. L., & Strutzel, E. (1968). The discovery of grounded theory; strategies for qualitative research. *Nursing Research, 17*(4), 364.

Goldkuhl, G., & Cronholm, S. (2010). Adding theoretical grounding to grounded theory: Toward multi-grounded theory. *International journal of qualitative methods, 9*(2), 187-205.

Gullino, P., & Larcher, F. (2012). Integrity in UNESCO World Heritage Sites. A comparative study for rural landscapes. *Journal of Cultural Heritage*. doi: http://dx.doi.org/10.1016/j.culher.2012.10.005

Mannay, D., & Morgan, M. (2014). Doing ethnography or applying a qualitative technique? Reflections from the 'waiting field'. *Qualitative Research,* 15(2)166-182.

Mehl, M. R., Gosling, S. D., & Pennebaker, J. W. (2006). Personality in its natural habitat: manifestations and implicit folk theories of personality in daily life. *Journal of personality and social psychology, 90*(5), 862.

Miles, M. B. Huberman, A. M., & Saldaña, J. (2013). *Qualitative data analysis:* A methods sourcebook: SAGE Publications, Inc. Thousand Oaks: London.

Muhammad, I. B., (2017). *Cultural Landscape Transactions and Values of a Nupe Community in Central Nigeria.* Delaware ,United States, Vernon Press.

Muhammad, I. B., & Said, I. (2015). Behavioural use of courtyard in a Nupe cultural landscape of Nigeria *Interdisciplinary Behaviour and Social Sciences* (pp. 227-232): CRC Press.

Muhammad, I. B., & Said, I. (2015). Spatial Transactions and Vernacular Architecture of a Nupe Community in Central Nigeria. *Jurnal Teknologi, 77*(15), 1-7.

Murchison, J. (2010). *Ethnography essentials: Designing, conducting and presenting your research* (Vol. 25): John Wiley and Sons: San Francisco.

Nadel, S. F. (1937). Gunnu, a Fertility Cult of the Nupe in Northern Nigeria. *Journal of the Anthropological Institute of Great Britain and Ireland,* 91-130.

Nadel, S. F. (1942). *A black Byzantium: the kingdom of Nupe in Nigeria:* International Institute of African languages & cultures, Oxford University Press: Cambridge.

Nassauer, J. I. (1995). Culture and changing landscape structure. *Landscape ecology, 10*(4), 229-237.

O'Reilly, K. (2009). *Key concepts in ethnography.* London: SAGE Publications Limited.

Patton, M. Q. (1987). *How to use qualitative methods in evaluation,* Sage Publication: London.

Patton, M. Q. (2005). *Qualitative research:* Wiley Online Library.

R Rapoport, A. (1969). *House Form and Culture. Foundations of cultural geography series.* Englewood Cliffs, New Jersey.

Risjord, M. (2007). Ethnography and culture. In S. P (Ed.), *Handbook of the Philosophy of Science. Philosophy of Anthropology and Sociology* (pp. 399-428): Elsevier B.V.

Seamon, D. (2009). Place, placelessness, insideness, and outsideness in John Sayles' Sunshine State. *The Journal of Media Geography,* 3, 1-19.

Seamon, D. (2014). Looking at a photograph – André Kertész's 1928 Meudon: Interpreting Aesthetic Experience Phenomenologically. *Academic Quarter* Vol 9, 4-18.

Seamon, D. (2015). Situated cognition and the phenomenology of place: life-world, environmental embodiment, and immersion-in-world. *Cognitive processing, 16*(1), 389-392.

Seamon, D., & Sowers, J. (2008). Place and placelessness, Edward Relph. *Key texts in Human Geography* 43-51.

Shopes, L. (2011). *Oral history. The Sage Handbook of Qualitative Research*, 451-465. Thousand Oaks: Califormia.

Stephenson, J. (2010). The dimensional landscape model: exploring differences in expressing and locating landscape qualities. *Landscape Research, 35*(3), 299-318.

Tengberg, A., Fredholm, S., Eliasson, I., Knez, I., Saltzman, K., & Wetterberg, O. (2012). Cultural ecosystem services provided by landscapes: Assessment of heritage values and identity. *Ecosystem services* 2, 14-26.

Türkyılmaz, Ç. C. (2016). Interrelated Values of Cultural Landscapes of Human Settlements: Case of Istanbul. *Procedia-Social and Behavioural Sciences, 222*, 502-509.

United-Nations. (2002). *United Nations New Agenda for the Development of Africa in the 1990s.* (A/57/304). Abuja Nigeria.

United Nations. (2016). Preparatory Committee for the United Nations Conference on Housing and Sustainable Urban Development (Habitat III). (A/CONF.226/PC.3/4).

WHC. (1994). *Convention Concerning the Protection of the World Cultural and Natural Heritage: World Heritage Committee, Seventh Session, Cartagena, Colombia, 6-11 December 1993: Report.* UNESCO.

Chapter 7

Conclusion:
Dimensions in the measure
of people-space relationships

[1]Isa Bala Muhammad and [2]Abubakar Danladi Isah

Department of Architecture, School of Environmental Technology,

Federal University of Technology, Minna, Nigeria

[1]*mib@futminna.edu.ng*

[2]*arcmuzaifa@futminna.edu.ng*

The continuous evaluation of people and space remains a phenomenon whose dimension has gained closer focus of the UN's sustainable development goals. The United Nations has recognised the undue neglect of indigenous people, their land, territories and resources. It recommends the recognition of indigenous people's issue as key towards the attainment of sustainable development goals. Thus, through the Permanent Forum on Indigenous Peoples' Issues, the UN has emphasised recognition and regard for the conservation of indigenous peoples' right to land, territories and resources. As a result, subjects related to Indigenous peoples' relationships with their root as a basis of their mainstream cultural, spiritual and social values for which their traditional knowledge systems were built and which determined their physical and economic well-being requires research (UN, 2018). Moreover, the UN sustainability indicators are found to lack adequate integration with positive and negative impacts of human interactions on sustainable development hence the need for discrete measurement tools for specific sustainable development issues (Brandon and Lombardi, 2011). In view of the foregone, identifying appropriate research procedures or a lead to it becomes paramount to social scientists.

The scientific procedure for the conduct of research in people and space transactions is characterised with a plethora of approaches which most of the time could be confusing especially to a beginner researcher. However, this book showcases five (5) different research methods conducted in different contexts of people and space transactions. Significantly, this book provides illustrative dimensions in the measurement of people and space interactions in the built environment towards responsive development. This covers the consideration of different settings of the built environment that include mountainous landscapes, urban neighbourhoods, hospital built environments, public housing settings and a cultural landscape of a typical rural ethnic community. These settings are influenced by culture and technology in space optimisation, linking urban dynamics with mainstream indigenous cultural and social values in both tangible and intangible expressions.

Consequently, a multidimensional data collection strategy has been established as more suitable for measuring people and space relationships in the built environment. Also, a time horizon where measurement of people and space transactions are assessed based on time scale was found to be essential in explicit and responsive research in the built environment. For example, this is shown in the study of "human wellbeing in mountain landscape environment employed multiple" measurement strategies that combines both subjective and objective measures as represented in Figure 7.1.

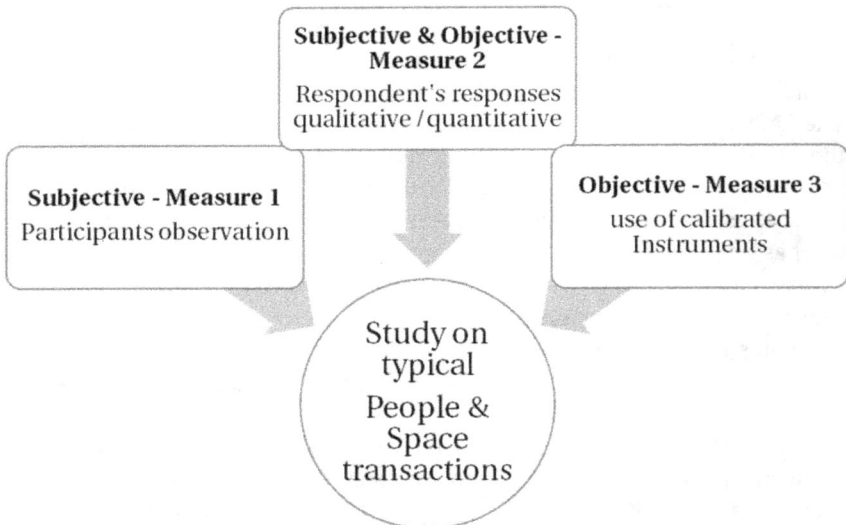

Figure 7.1 The use of Multi-dimension strategies in the collection of data

The objectives of a study determine what and how research information is sought and measured (Yin, 2013). As showcased in Figure 7.1, the same study had three of its objectives measured differently towards the attainment of the research goal.

It is also important for the researcher to establish a philosophical stance in a people-place relationship. Exemplifying this is Chapter 4 where the researcher chose a philosophical stance of pragmatism. This is because the research objectives required the consideration of both subjective and objective measures and as such pragmatism was chosen as the philosophical stance- a middle ground between constructivism and positivism.

Equally important is the underpinning of constructs of measure based on literature. Such underpinning of research constructs does not necessarily have to be exactly the same but similarities in the factors to be measured could serve as a good reason for adoption. It is however required that an overview of the dimensions is presented and thereafter an appropriate measure in the context of the study is established. Contrastingly, explorative research such as ethnography may pose some challenges in the underpinning of measures, because most of the findings are likely to be inductive as well as grounded on data (Mannay & Morgan, 2014). It is therefore required that strategies are employed towards reliability and validity in the collection of data. Appropriately, this book showcased five (5) different research dimensions on the strategies for validity and reliability of measures towards responsive sustainable development.

Most importantly, these studies utilised outstanding strategies in their methodologies which makes the researches unique, original and thus contributing to the broad knowledge of research methodology in different ways. Significantly it shows that measure of people and space transactions in particular and qualitatively dominated research studies, in general, requires dynamic approach in the dimensions of measure with each case study developing new and unique strategies based on the field situation and the phenomenon being examined.

Beyond these, this book achieved one of its cardinal objectives by innovatively establishing an overtly meaningful assessment platform where both experts and the lay public share value systems underlying criteria and performance in people and space transactions through multiple methods.

In sum, this book provides direction in social science research methodology built on evidence-based scientific inquiry of the built environment which can guide young researchers in projecting methods for social research problems. It is also a foundation of methodological template for seasoned researchers to explore options in research process innovation. A significant deduction that is drawn from the methodological approaches are that first each investigation needs to be established on a philosophical stance and this goes a long way in determining the type of data to be collected, analysed and interpreted. This means that the nature of research should not be methodologically led but rather philosophically led.

References

Brandon P. S. & Lombardi P. (2011). *Evaluating Sustainable Development in the Built Environment*, Wiley-Blackwell, John Wiley and Sons: United Kingdom.

Mannay, D. & Morgan, M. (2014). Doing ethnography or applying a qualitative technique? Reflections from the 'waiting field'. *Qualitative Research*, 1468794113517391.

United Nations, (2018). Permanent Forum on Indigenous Issues. Economic and Social Council Official Records, 2018. A report on the seventeenth session Supplement No. 23, (E/2018/43-E/C.19/2018/11)

Yin, R. K. (2013). *Case Study Research: Design and methods*, Sage publications: Thousand Oaks, California.

Index